Batsford Chess Library

The Guide to Chess

Malcolm Pein

An Owl Book
Henry Holt and Company
New York

Henry Holt and Company, Inc.
Publishers since 1866
115 West 18th Street
New York, New York 10011

Henry Holt® is a registered
trademark of Henry Holt and Company, Inc.

Published in Canada by Fitzhenry & Whiteside Ltd.,
195 Allstate Parkway, Markham, Ontario L3R 4R8.

First published in the United States in 1995 by
Henry Holt and Company, Inc.
Originally published in Great Britain in 1995 by
B. T. Batsford Ltd.

Library of Congress Catalog Card Number: 95-79224

ISBN 0-8050-4225-3 (An Owl Book: pbk.)

First American Edition—1995

Printed in the United Kingdom
All first editions are printed on acid-free paper.∞

10   9   8   7   6   5   4   3   2   1

Editorial Panel: Mark Dvoretsky, John Nunn, Jon Speelman
General Adviser: Raymond Keene OBE
Managing Editor: Graham Burgess

Contents

Symbols

+	Check
++	Double check
x	Capture
!!	Excellent move
!	Good move
!?	Interesting move
?!	Dubious move
?	Bad move
??	Blunder
OL	Olympiad
Ch	Championship
Z	Zonal
jr	Junior event
wom	Women's event
mem	Memorial event
sim	Simultaneous game
rpd	Rapidplay game
Corr	Postal game
(*n*)	*n*th match game

Many other symbols are used in more specialised literature. Here is a useful list of those you are likely to encounter:

±±	White is winning
±	White is much better
⩲	White is slightly better
=	Equal position
⩱	Black is slightly better
∓	Black is much better
∓∓	Black is winning
∞	The position is unclear
∞	White has compensation
∞	Black has compensation
↑	With initiative
⇄	With counterplay
⊡	Bishop pair
⊕	Time trouble
Δ	Intending ...
□	Only move
⌒	Better is ...
«	Queenside
»	Kingside
⊞	Centre
×	Weakness

Foreword

Chess has been likened to:

Life – by Bobby Fischer, the one chess player everyone has heard of, World Champion 1972-75.

Science – by Mikhail Botvinnik, World Champion 1948-57, 1958-1960, 1961-63.

War – by Emanuel Lasker, World Champion 1894-1921.

Art – by Fred Reinfeld, an American chess writer.

Various sports, political negotiations, and lots of other things – by journalists who have never played chess.

A day at the office – by Jon Speelman, a professional chess player and one of England's top grandmasters, who as far as I know has never had a 9 to 5 job.

Football, but only the midfield – by your scribe who was born in Liverpool and spent many of his formative years at the Kop end.

Watching paint dry – by a *Guardian* journalist – but who cares? This is *The Daily Telegraph* Guide to Chess.

Chess is, to most people who play it, above all a fun pastime and an endless challenge. Chess is universal; there are no age, social or language barriers. You can play against your next-door neighbour or an opponent on the other side of the world.

It is of proven educational value to schoolchildren developing logical thinking and concentration.

This guide will teach you the rules and basic strategies. Once you have grasped them there is plenty of information on the chess world, where to play and how to improve your game.

Chess is easy to learn yet there are more possibilities than any number of computers will ever be able to calculate. All we can do is scratch the surface here but I hope you will be enthused sufficiently to explore some more.

Acknowledgements

To my researcher Jonathan Wilson, without whom this book would have been several years, rather than several months late.

To Graham Burgess of Batsford, for burning the midnight oil.

To my father, who, as my mother once wryly remarked, did not cook for me, wash me, dress me or take me to school but simply taught me chess, which turned out to be much more useful.

Malcolm Pein
Daily Telegraph Chess Correspondent
London 1995

1   The Rules of Chess

Chess is a game of skill for two players, known as White and Black, each commanding an army of 16 pieces on an 8x8 chequered board. The players take turns to move, White making the first move of the game. Unlike cricket, where a team may forfeit its innings to have more time to bowl out the opposition, in chess the player whose turn it is to move *must do something* – this obligation to move can sometimes be very costly. The object of the game is to checkmate the opponent's king. What this means, and how best to go about it, is the subject of much of this book...

The initial position

The diagram above shows the chessboard set up for the start of play. Each player has an identical force of 1 king, 1 queen, 2 bishops, 2 knights, 2 rooks and 8 pawns. In all

chess diagrams, White plays 'up' the board, unless stated otherwise.

A common mistake in setting up the board is to get the king and queen the wrong way round. Remember that the board is always placed with a light square at White's bottom right-hand corner, and the queens stand on squares of their own colour.

The columns of squares are known as 'files', and named by the letters 'a' to 'h', while the rows are called 'ranks' and numbered from 1 to 8. Just as in an A to Z map, each square is identified by a unique grid reference, for example 'g4'. Collectively, the e- to h-files and a- to d-files are known as the kingside and queenside respectively, in deference to the initial positions of the monarchs.

The squares e4, d4, d5 and e5 are known as *the centre* and they are of great significance as will become apparent. Most of the pieces have a much greater range from the centre compared with the edge of the board. In chess as in football, control of the midfield is a big step towards victory.

The Centre

The pieces and their moves

The rook

The rook moves in straight lines, horizontally and vertically. Like any other piece, it can either move to a vacant square, or capture an opposing piece. A capture is executed by moving the capturing piece to the square where its victim stands, and removing this captured piece from the board.

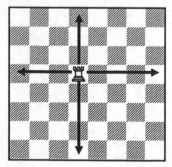

On an empty board, the rook is unique in that it is equally mobile wherever it stands, covering 14 squares.

Inexperienced players often call the rook a 'castle' – this is incorrect and should be discouraged, if only because it's a sure way to show off your inexperience!

The bishop

The bishop moves diagonally, as shown in the diagram.

From a central square such as d4, the bishop can cover its maximum of 13 squares, but in a corner its influence is reduced to 7 squares.

The bishop is the only piece that is restricted to squares of one colour. The two bishops can often be a potent attacking force.

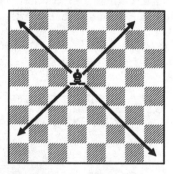

The queen

The queen is like a rook and a bishop rolled into one. It moves any number of squares horizontally, vertically and diagonally.

On an empty board, a queen on d4 covers an unprecedented 27 squares, and controls 21 squares even from the corner.

The queen is the most powerful piece on the board; look after it.

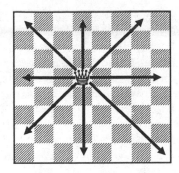

The knight

The knight moves in an 'L' shape, as shown below. Nothing can stand in its way, as it simply jumps over any pieces standing between itself and its destination.

A knight in the centre attacks eight squares, but a knight in the corner covers only two. All of my junior pupils know the rhyme 'a knight on the rim is dim'.

The knight is the only piece capable of jumping over other pieces, and the only piece not to move in straight lines.

The pawn

The pawn's basic move is a modest one square forwards. However, on its first move of the game, each pawn has the right – but by no means any obligation – to move two squares forward. The pawn captures one square *diagonally* forwards.

The pawn is the only piece to move in one way and capture in another. It is also the only piece that can never move backwards – so consider each pawn move carefully.

Special moves

There are two more exotic features of the pawn's move: promotion and the *en passant* capture.

Pawn promotion

If a pawn succeeds in advancing all the way to the far end of the board (i.e. the eighth rank for a white pawn) its bravery is rewarded with a promotion. On being played to the 8th rank, the pawn is removed from the board and a piece of the player's choice takes its place on the promoting square – all in one turn. In the overwhelming majority of cases a queen will be chosen, and so pawn promotion is commonly referred to as 'queening'. But it is important to remember that 'underpromotion' to rook, bishop or knight is always a possibility, and will occasionally be the strongest move.

If your original queen is still on the board when you promote, you are perfectly entitled to claim a second queen – in fact, if one player managed to promote all of his pawns, he could have nine queens on the board at once! If you are lucky enough to acquire a second queen in tournament play, it should be possible to borrow one from a nearby board where play has finished. If you are playing at home and do not have another set, a rook turned upside-down is the usual substitute.

Unfortunately, you may not promote to a king, or to a piece of the opposing colour – this loophole in the laws was closed many years ago. On promoting a pawn, you must decide immediately which new piece you want. There is no question of waiting for a move or two to see what happens!

En passant

This special case of the pawn capture remains a mystery to many novice players, and has been the subject of some very heated arguments! The rule is as follows:

If a pawn moves two squares forwards, and in so doing passes over a square that is under attack from an enemy pawn, it can be captured *en passant* – 'in passing' – just as if it had moved only one square. The *en passant* capture is only possible on the next move: it must be made immediately, or not at all.

The king

The king can move in any direction, but only one square at a time. He may not move to any square that is attacked by an opposing piece.

Check

If the king is attacked by an enemy piece, he is said to be 'in check'. When a player is in check, he must use his next move to get out of check; in addition, it is illegal to make a move that places one's own king in check.

The queen gives check

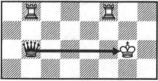

In principle, there are three ways to escape a check:

1) Capture the piece giving check.

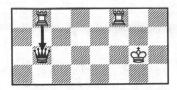

2) Block the check – shield the king by moving some other piece into the attacker's line of fire.

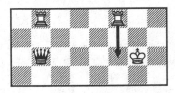

3) move the king to a safe square.

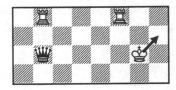

If none of the above is possible, it is 'checkmate' and the game is over.

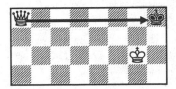

Checkmate

The word 'checkmate' is derived from the Arabic 'shah mat', which literally means 'the king is dead'. Checkmate is achieved precisely when the king is in check and there is no way to escape from check.

The king is never actually captured – while he may be happy for the rest of his army to fight to the last drop of blood, he signs the humiliating peace treaty just in time to save his own skin.

In master chess, it is unusual for a game to end in checkmate. A strong player usually knows when he has no hope of averting checkmate in the long run. When he feels he has passed the point of no return, he will normally resign, and spare himself and his opponent the trouble of playing the game out to the bitter end. This is exactly equivalent to a snooker player conceding the frame when he needs some improbable number of snookers to catch up. In chess, as in snooker, to continue in such a situation could be seen as disrespectful to the opponent in a game between two experienced players. Until you have mastered all the instructions in this book, follow the adage 'no one ever won a game by resigning'. The cause of resignation in a grandmaster game is often a mystery to beginners or even experienced players. I always try to include some explanation in my *Daily Telegraph* columns although space does not always permit. This explanation of a chess game is known as 'analysis' and is composed of 'variations'. There will be plenty of analysis later in this book.

Stalemate

If, on a player's turn to move, he is not in check but has no legal move, then he is in stalemate and the game is a draw.

We often hear on the news that political negotiations, for example, have reached a 'stalemate'. This usage is rather inaccurate: political 'stalemates' are often no more than temporary hitches, which are resolved when the protagonists agree either to make concessions or to fight. In the logical world of chess, there is no possibility to continue once a stalemate has arisen − the stalemated player is obliged to make a move but there is no move he can legally play!

The use of inappropriate chess analogies by writers, particularly sports journalists, has reached epidemic proportions of late, even in *The Daily Telegraph*. Getting irritated by them is an occupational hazard of being a chess player but one classic really stands out, heard on BBC's snooker coverage after a good shot for position − "snooker, it's like chess with balls". For a fabulously witty and detailed rebuttal of this absurd proposition written by Grandmaster Jonathan Levitt send me an SAE c/o *The Daily Telegraph* − but I digress, there is one special move we must examine without delay; it could save your skin every game.

Castling

This is a special case of the king's move, and it is the only chance you get to move two pieces in one go. The basic mechanism of castling is this: the king moves two squares

sideways, the rook jumps over and stands alongside.

Pieces on starting squares.

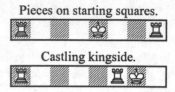

Castling kingside.

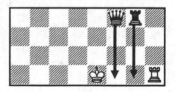

Castling is a special privilege, and is only allowed under certain conditions.

1) All the squares between king and rook must be vacant.

2) The king and rook with which you wish to castle must not have moved earlier in the game, and it follows that they must be on their initial squares. Once a king or rook moves, it forfeits the right to castle for good, even if it returns to its initial square.

3) It is illegal to castle to escape a check. It is also impossible to castle 'into' check (i.e. the king's destination square is attacked) or 'through' check (the king's intermediate square is under fire).

A consequence of rule '2' is that you may only castle once in a game. Nevertheless, the heat of the battle occasionally gets the better of players, and some absent-minded masters have been known to castle illegally or even twice in the same game!

It is possible to castle either on the kingside ('short' castling) or queenside ('long' castling), but remember that the king always moves two squares. Newcomers to chess have been known to attempt queenside castling by moving the king to b1 and rook to c1, but this is quite wrong.

Pieces on starting squares.

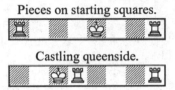

Castling queenside.

In castling, the king is moved first, and then the rook; if you try to castle moving the rook first, you risk falling foul of the 'touch move' rule, and being forced to move only your rook.

The 'touch move' rule

An important part of chess etiquette is the 'touch move' rule. This states simply that if a player touches a piece, he has to move it. However, there is no penalty if the touched piece turns out to have no legal move. A move is completed when the player's hand leaves the piece, and he may not attempt to retract the move after this moment.

The sole exception to the touch move rule occurs when a player wants to adjust the position of a piece on its square. In this case, he should say 'J'adoube' (or its English equivalent, 'I adjust') before making the adjustment. He should only do this when it is his own turn to move.

Illegal moves

There is no specific penalty for making an illegal move, but the touch move rule still applies. If an illegal move is made, but passes unnoticed until some time later in the game, play should return to the position in which the illegal move was played. If the mistake is not spotted until after the game is finished, however, the result of the game must stand.

Drawn games

There are a variety of ways in which a game can be drawn.

1) Threefold repetition

A draw by repetition can be claimed if the same position arises three times during a game with the same player to move in each case. The repetitions need not be consecutive, although they usually are. Sameness of position is defined by sameness of available moves – even if all the pieces stand on the same squares, the loss of the right to castle or to capture *en passant* would constitute a change in the position.

2) Perpetual check

A draw by perpetual check occurs when one player gives a series of checks from which his opponent can never escape. This is really a special case of the draw by repetition, as any perpetual sequence of checks must be repeatable at least three times!

3) Insufficient mating material

The game is drawn if neither side has sufficient pieces remaining to give checkmate. The endings of

KvK, K+NvK and K+BvK are drawn automatically for this reason.

4) Stalemate

The player to move is not in check, but has no legal move – as discussed above.

5) The 50 move rule

If 50 consecutive moves are played (by each side) without a pawn being moved or a capture being made, a draw can be claimed under the 50 move rule. The purpose of this rule is to save players from being tortured indefinitely by an opponent who is unable to force a win but reluctant to agree a draw. Fifty moves is an arbitrary choice of cut-off point. At the time the rule was introduced, it seemed fair enough to suppose that if the superior side can't win in that amount of time, he never will. However, research using massive computer databases revealed positions where a win can be forced, with no captures or pawn moves for more than 50 moves. However, the chance of any human possessing the necessary technique to achieve such a feat is negligible, and after some consternation, the 50 move rule has remained in place.

Chess Notation

1) Algebraic Notation

The 'algebraic' system is the simplest and most concise method of chess notation, and is used worldwide. Each square is named according to the scheme described above, while the king, queen, rook and bishop are represented by 'K', 'Q', 'R', and 'B'. The knight is denoted by 'N', and the humble pawn is not named at all!

The symbols 'x' and '+' denote a capture and check respectively; these are used when appropriate, if desired – some publications leave them out altogether. In Batsford books they are always included.

In *The Daily Telegraph* I use x and +. Occasionally they may be omitted if they make the move more than five characters long and overrun the width of a column!

Pawn moves are represented simply by naming the square the pawn moves to, e.g. 'd6'; an exception is made for pawn captures, when the pawn is named by the file it has come from, e.g. 'cxd6'.

If the move played could have been made by another piece, we avoid ambiguity by naming the file the piece came from. For example, if White plays his rook from f1 to d1, but he also has a rook on a1 that could have made the same move, we write 'Rfd1'.

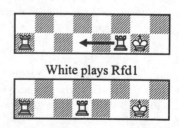

White plays Rfd1

If the pieces concerned are on the same file, we use the rank number instead, for example 'N1d2'.

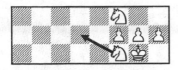

White plays N1d2

Castling kingside is written '0-0', and castling queenside '0-0-0'. In the event of a pawn promoting, an '=' sign (optional) and the symbol for the new piece is added after the destination square, e.g. 'd8=Q+' or just 'd8Q+', etc., the latter being the standard Batsford format. Checkmate is normally indicated by '#'; curiously, there is no symbol for stalemate.

A variation on this, which some people find helpful when they are learning the algebraic notation, is 'long' algebraic. In this system, the square a piece moves from is specified as well e.g. Ng1-f3.

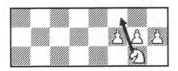

Long notation:
White plays Ng1-f3

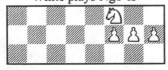

This heads off any question of ambiguity, but it is less economical than standard algebraic. In long algebraic, the sample moves given above would be written 'c5xd6', 'Ra1-d1' and so on.

In his column in the Weekend *Telegraph* GM David Norwood uses figurine long algebraic with a picture instead of a letter for the piece and both departure and destination squares, e.g. ♘g1-f3. Unfortunately in my daily column the page format determines that I must employ 'short algebraic'.

2) Descriptive Notation

Although descriptive notation was in standard usage in Britain and the United States until fairly recently, it has come to symbolise everything the non-chess-playing public find mysterious and confusing about the game. In any case, it could only find favour in those countries where 12 inches make a foot, 3 feet make a yard, and 1760 yards make a mile! Although descriptive notation is fast becoming obsolete, it is as well to be 'bilingual', as many classic books still await 'translation' into algebraic.

The basis of the descriptive notation is that each file is named after the piece that starts the game there, so the e-file, for example, is known as the king's file – K-file for short. A square is identified by counting the number of squares it is 'up' the file – but seen from the player's own point of view. Therefore the square e4 is White's K4, but Black's K5.

In contrast to the algebraic system, the pawn *is* named – 'P', naturally enough – and some old books use 'Kt' to represent the knight.

Ambiguities are resolved, in the first instance, by prefixing either 'Q' or 'K' to the names of files and/or pieces as and when appropriate – so the a- and h-files are known as the QR- and KR-files respectively. Checks and *en passant* captures (marked 'e.p.') are not optional but an integral part of the notation – 'PxP' and 'PxP+' are different moves, not alternative ways to write the same move. Anyone using this system has to navigate carefully between the twin perils of ambiguity and redundancy: every time you make a move on one side of the board, say Bg5, you must check whether its mirror image (i.e. Bb5) is possible! If so, you must write 'B-KN5'; if not, only 'B-N5' is correct.

When a game is written down, the white and black moves are paired off, and the move number always refers to the number of moves made by White.

You can test your knowledge of chess notation by playing through the following game.

Rosanes-Anderssen
Breslau 1862

Algebraic		Descriptive	
1 e4	e5	1 P-K4	P-K4
2 f4	d5	2 P-KB4	P-Q4
3 exd5	e4	3 KPxP	P-K5
4 Bb5+	c6	4 B-N5+	P-B3
5 dxc6	Nxc6	5 PxP	NxP
6 Nc3	Nf6	6 N-QB3	N-B3
7 Qe2	Bc5	7 Q-K2	B-QB4

8 Nxe4	0-0	8 NxP	0-0
9 Bxc6	bxc6	9 BxN	PxB
10 d3	Re8	10 P-Q3	R-K1
11 Bd2	Nxe4	11 B-Q2	NxN
12 dxe4	Bf5	12 PxN	B-B4
13 e5	Qb6	13 P-K5	Q-N3
14 0-0-0	Bd4	14 0-0-0	B-Q5
15 c3	Rab8	15 P-B3	QR-N1
16 b3	Red8	16 P-QN3	KR-Q1
17 Nf3		17 N-B3	

White misses the threat, although 17 Kb2 Be6 (17 K-N2 B-K3) threatens the unstoppable 18...Bxb3 (18...BxP). Note the '...'; this is the conventional way to indicate a move by Black.

17 ...	Qxb3	17 ...	QxP
18 axb3	Rxb3	18 PxQ	RxP
19 Be1	Be3+	19 B-K1	B-K6+
20 Resigns		20 Resigns	

Any white move is met by 20...Rb1 mate (20...R-N8 mate).

Virtually all chess publications nowadays use the 'figurine algebraic' notation; this is simply the standard algebraic notation with the pieces denoted by icons (figurines) instead of initial letters.

K = ♔
Q = ♕
R = ♖
B = ♗
N = ♘

This chess language is understood in every country in the world, and will be used in the rest of this book.

If you have absorbed all of the above you can now play a legal game of chess. The next few chapters are devoted to ensuring that you can win a few games.

2 Tactics

"To free your game, take off some of your adversary's men, if possible for nothing" – Captain Bertin, *The Noble Game of Chess* (1735)

Introduction

The elements of chess skill fall into two broad categories: 'strategy' and 'tactics'. Strategy is the process of identifying the most important long-term features of a position, and forming a general plan as appropriate. This would be quite sufficient if our opponent could be relied on to shuffle around aimlessly – but in practice he is more likely to be fighting tooth and nail to cut across our strategy and implement his own! The question of whether we can play the moves we would like to is decided by tactics – that is, the calculation of exact sequences of moves.

In this chapter, we will look at the elementary devices from which all tactical play is composed.

The relative value of the pieces

We have already looked at the relative merits of the pieces on an empty board in the first chapter. While this may be of theoretical interest, how do we decide whether to exchange our queen for a rook and bishop in an actual game? A convenient, if rather crude, solution is to give each piece a numerical value according to the following scheme:

Queen	9 points
Rook	5
Bishop	3
Knight	3
Pawn	1

The player whose army is worth more 'points' is said to have a 'material' advantage; other things being equal, an advantage of just one 'point' should be sufficient to win.

One the most important endgames to master is that of king and pawn v king, knowing when it is a win and when it is a draw and how to convert your one point or one pawn advantage. It follows that material balance is very important, but try not to overestimate its importance: there are many situations in which other considerations take precedence – not least a mating attack!

Norwood-Marsh
Walsall 1992

1 ♕xc6+!! ♔xc6 2 ♘xd4++ ♔b6
3 ♖b1+ ♔a6 4 ♗b7+ ♔a5 5 ♗d2+

♔a4 6 ♗c6+ ♔xa3 7 ♗c1+ ♔a2 8 ♖b2+ ♔a1 9 ♘c2#

The moral of the story is that there is more to chess than mere point-scoring. 'Points' in chess are imaginary: they measure the armies' relative strength in some idealised, 'average' position. Average chess positions are seen as often as families with 2.4 children!

The elements of chess tactics

The simple attack

The simplest tactic of all is to spot an undefended enemy piece and attack it! If your opponent misses the threat, allowing his piece to be taken for free (or exchanged for a piece of lesser value), it is said to have been left *'en prise'* or 'hanging'.

Perhaps the most dreadful blunder of all is to allow Fool's Mate:

Fool's Mate
1 f3? e5 2 g4?? ♛h4#

Yes, it's possible to be checkmated in two moves — but only if you're an absolute fool! The king's safety is of paramount importance, but White's rash pawn moves have left him helpless against the attack down the e1-h4 diagonal.

The Fork

A simultaneous attack by one piece on two enemy units is called a 'fork' — an appropriate image might involve the hapless victims impaled on the prongs of a pitchfork! Many people's first experience of the fork goes something like this:

1 e4 e5 2 ♘f3 ♘c6 3 ♗c4 ♘f6 4 ♘g5 d6?? 5 ♘xf7

The knight simultaneously attacks — or *forks* — the queen and rook.

Scholar's Mate

This both illustrates the idea we are examining, the fork, and is something you are bound to come across sooner rather than later.

1 e4 e5 2 ♗c4 ♗c5

2...♘f6 is a good move.

3 ♛h5

The white queen forks e5 and f7 and if 3...g6, 4 ♛xe5+ checks the king and attacks the rook on h8, another fork.

Black sees a chance to develop a piece with gain of time, but he saves even more time than he anticipates.

3...♘f6??

Black should play 3...♛e7!.

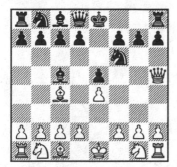

4 ♛xf7#

Literally thousands of games have ended this way.

This is known as Scholar's Mate, possibly because bright schoolchildren have been landing it on their friends, parents and teachers for five hundred years! I was taught the game by my father at the age of three. He taught me how to play 'properly'; in his world no one would be so crude as to try this simple attack. Two years later I played my first competitive tournament, The Under-7 Championship in the Liverpool Junior Congress, at the time the biggest junior event in the world. In the first round I lost exactly as above and burst into tears. A friendly teacher realised I must have some promise because I was the only child who brought a pen and wrote the moves down. She showed how to avoid the quick mate with a simple developing move and I won my next 16 games and took the title.

Sometimes a fork can be employed for purely positional gains; the 'fork trick' below is an excellent way to break up an enemy pawn centre.

Lechtynsky-Sax
Tallinn 1979
1 e4 d6 2 d4 ♘f6 3 ♘c3 g6 4 ♗c4 ♗g7 5 ♘f3 0-0 6 0-0

Notionally White's two pawns in the centre give him an advantage but this can be neutralised using a fork.

6...♘xe4 7 ♘xe4 d5

The d5-pawn forks the bishop and knight ensuring the return of the sacrificed knight.

8 ♗d3 dxe4 9 ♗xe4 ♘d7 and Black has a satisfactory position.

The Pin

A piece which shields another, more valuable, piece from an enemy attack is said to be 'pinned'. The pin is an important tactical weapon because the reduced mobility of a pinned piece very often renders it powerless to help either its colleagues or itself. The following game shows how to set up and exploit a pin to great effect.

Spielmann-Wahle
Vienna 1926

1 e4 e6 2 d4 d5 3 ♘c3 ♘f6 4 exd5 exd5 5 ♗g5 ♗e7 6 ♗d3 ♘c6 7 ♘ge2

7 ♘f3 would allow 7...♗g4, with a more irritating pin – since the bishop has already moved once, he would not want to play it back to e2 to break the pin.

7...♘b4 8 ♘g3 ♘xd3+ 9 ♕xd3 g6?

10 0-0 c6 11 ♖ae1

The rook pins the bishop to the king; the bishop cannot move else the black king would be in check. Now 11 ♗xf6 is a serious threat: the bishop on e7 would be powerless to recapture. Black should block the e-file with 11...♗e6, but he fails to sense the danger.

11...0-0 12 ♖xe7!

This sets up a new pin, which really is fatal.

12...♕xe7

The f6-knight is now pinned by the g5-bishop to the queen on e7.

13 ♕f3 ♔g7

13...♗f5 14 ♘xf5 gxf5 15 ♕g3 ♔g7 (15...♔h8 16 ♕h4 ♔g7 17 ♕h6+ ♔g8 18 ♗xf6) 16 ♗xf6+

♔xf6 17 ♕h4+ ♔e6 18 ♖e1+ ♔d7 19 ♕xe7+ wins the house.

14 ♘ce4!

Spielmann wastes no time in putting the boot in.

14...dxe4 15 ♘xe4

15...♕e6

At least this escapes the fork after 16 ♗xf6+. Instead, after 15...♕xe4, 16 ♗xf6+ wins the queen, but 16 ♕xf6+ ♔g8 17 ♗h6 forces checkmate. None of this would have been possible without the reckless 9...g6.

16 ♗xf6+ ♔g8

16...♔h6 17 ♕f4+ mates on g5 next move.

17 ♕f4 1-0

Black can only prevent 18 ♕h6 and 19 ♕g7# by giving up his queen.

There are many ways to prevent a pin wreaking such havoc:

1) Block the pin using a less valuable piece

This is the least disruptive way to counter a pin, and probably the most common.

1 d4 d5 2 c4 e6 3 ♘c3 ♘f6 4 ♗g5

A very common position from the Queen's Gambit, White's last move pins the f6-knight.

4...♗e7

Black develops a piece, prepares castling and breaks the pin.

2) Exchange or drive away the pinning piece

In the example we have just seen, the bishop on g5 is pinning the knight on f6; if it moves away the black queen would be captured by the white bishop.

A common mechanism here is the ...h6, ...g5 pawn advance. If you have castled kingside, or intend to, don't make this advance without a very good reason, as it could seriously weaken your king's position. Watch out for a ♘xg5 sacrifice smashing your king's defences – an example is given below.

1 e4 e5 2 ♘f3 ♘c6 3 ♗c4 ♗c5 4 0-0 ♘f6 5 d3 d6 6 ♗g5 h6 7 ♗h4 g5

One of my favourite examples, Black breaks the pin and launches a counterattack.

8 ♗g3 h5! 9 ♘xg5 h4! 10 ♘xf7

A fork which wins material but does not save the game.

10...hxg3 11 ♘xd8

11 hxg3 ♕e7 12 ♘xh8 ♕h7 intending ...♘g4 and ...♕h2#.

11...♗g4 12 ♕d2 ♘d4 13 ♘c3 ♖xh2 14 ♘f7

14 fxg3 ♘f3# is a double discovered checkmate, but they come later in the chapter.

14...♘f3+ 15 gxf3 ♗xf3 and ♖h1 mate.

Also beware of a piece sacrifice to maintain the pin.

1 e4 e5 2 ♘f3 ♘c6 3 ♗c4 ♗c5 4 ♘c3 ♘f6 5 d3 d6 6 0-0 0-0 7 ♗g5 h6 8 ♗h4 a6 9 ♘d5

Threatening to smash open Black's kingside with a capture on f6. A recapture with the g7-pawn will leave the black king exposed.

9...g5

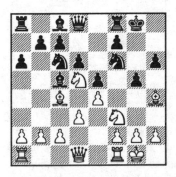

10 ♘xg5! hxg5 11 ♗xg5

The pin is even deadlier than before. Since 11...♘xd5 loses the queen, Black cannot prevent the capture of his knight.

3) Ignore the pin – putting the question

By this we mean allowing, or even provoking, the opponent to carry out his positional threat – typically to make a mess of our pawn structure.

1 d4 ♘f6 2 c4 e6 3 ♘c3 ♗b4

This bishop move introduces an opening called the Nimzo-Indian Defence. The naming of the openings will be discussed later.

4 a3

Asking the question to the bishop and claiming that the resultant doubling of White's pawns is no threat – actually rather a bold claim. The pin will be broken whatever the bishop does because the attempt to maintain the pin is flawed.

4...♗xc3+

4...♗a5 5 b4 ♗b6 6 c5 traps the bishop and wins it for a pawn.

5 bxc3

White will aim to prove that his game does not suffer due to the doubled c-pawns, and that Black has made a greater concession.

4) Play round the pin

If there is no threat to increase the pressure on the pinned piece, it may be desirable to keep our options open.

Nimzowitsch-Capablanca

1 e4 e5 2 ♘f3 ♘c6 3 ♗c4 ♗c5 4 ♘c3 ♘f6 5 d3 d6 6 ♗g5 ♗e6

6...h6 7 ♗xf6 ♕xf6 8 ♘d5 attacks the queen and the c7-pawn, but after the move played, 7 ♗xe6 fxe6 would favour Black, who has a strong central pawn mass and play down the half-open f-file.

7 ♗b5 h6 8 ♗h4 ♗b4

Capablanca sets up a pin of his own.

9 d4

Threatening d5 forking bishop and knight.

9...♗d7

Breaking the pin.

10 0-0

Capablanca now initiates a forcing sequence to break the pin. First of all, he must eliminate the knight before it reaches d5.

10...♗xc3 11 bxc3 g5

Finally breaking the second pin, because it enables the unpinned piece to capture the key e4-pawn.

12 ♗g3 ♘xe4

Black has a perfectly satisfactory position.

5) Escape – by any means necessary

Sometimes the pinned piece strikes back...

Legall-St Brie
Paris
1 e4 e5 2 ♗c4 d6 3 ♘f3 ♗g4 4 ♘c3 g6?? 5 ♘xe5! ♗xd1 6 ♗xf7+ ♔e7 7 ♘d5#

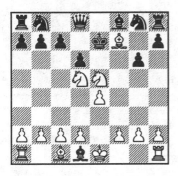

6) Avoid the pin

1 e4 e5 2 ♘f3 ♘c6 3 ♗b5 a6 4 ♗a4 ♘f6 5 0-0 ♗e7 6 ♖e1 b5 7 ♗b3 d6 8 c3 0-0 9 h3

Forestalling the pin 9...♗g4 which would hamper White's plan of d4.

The Skewer

The 'skewer' is a relative of the pin. Once again, two pieces stand in the firing line of an enemy man, but in this case the piece in immediate danger is of equal or greater value than its comrade. A skewer often wins material at once; even if it can be blocked, the blocking piece will be moving into a pin.

Chekhover, USSR Ch Bulletin 1945

1 ♕c5+!

Now and later on, the knight is immune since ...♔xe4 loses to the skewer ♕c2+. White makes repeated use of this tactic to drive the enemy king towards his own.

1...♔d3

Wherever the king moves, the black queen is lost, e.g. 1...♔xe4 2 ♕c2+.

2 ♕c3+ ♔e2 3 ♕d2+ ♔f3 4 ♕f2+

The knight is immune from capture because of the skewer idea.

4...♔g4 5 ♕g3+ ♔f5 6 ♘d6+

Now the mating net closes around the black king. 'Queen and knight, they're all right' is a good maxim – the two pieces complement each other. A queen aided by a bishop, a piece of equivalent strength to a knight is often not as powerful because the bishop does not have access to any squares that the queen cannot reach from the same square. In a sense the bishop is a subset of the queen but the knight has lots of extra possibilities to offer.

6...♔f6 7 ♘e8+ ♔f5 8 ♘g7+ ♔f6 9 ♕f4+ and mate next move.

Lutz-Piket
Wijk aan Zee 1995
A game between two top-flight grandmasters; they can blunder just as badly as the rest of us.

10 d4 cxd4 11 ♘xd4
Attacking the c6-pawn but Black ignores the threat.

11...♘e6! 12 ♘xc6?? ♕xd1 13 ♖xd1 ♗b7

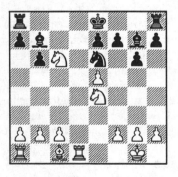

The knights are skewered. Any move of the attacked knight exposes the other to capture.

Discovered Attack
A 'discovered' attack occurs when one piece moves, uncovering an at-tack from one of its colleagues. This device can be highly potent if the moving piece attacks something as well — especially the king!

Vasiukov-Kholmov
Moscow 1964

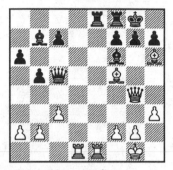

1 ♗xg7! ♗xg7 2 ♕h5
Threatening mate on h7.

2...h6 3 ♗h7+! and wins the queen.

Discovered Check and Double Check
A discovered attack on the king is called a discovered check. Since the opponent's first duty is to escape the check, the moving piece has a li-cence to kill! If the moving piece gives check *and* discovers check, the result is a double check.

Discovered check is the theme of a useful opening trap:
1 e4 e5 2 ♘f3 ♘f6 3 ♘xe5 ♘xe4
You cannot just copy your oppo-nent's moves in chess without allow-ing White a winning move sooner or later.

4 ♕e2 ♘f6 5 ♘c6+
Black must block the check and whichever way he does it, 5...♕e7 or

5...♗e7, the white knight captures the black queen.

This allegedly occurred in a game between two top grandmasters – Nigel Short (age 10) against *Daily Telegraph* chess columnist David Norwood then aged 6!

A double check is a strong forcing move, as it can only be answered by moving the king. Sometimes huge sacrifices can be made for the sake of a double check.

Réti-Tartakower
Vienna 1910
1 e4 c6 2 d4 d5 3 ♘c3 dxe4 4 ♘xe4 ♘f6 5 ♕d3 e5

Although the pawn can easily be recaptured, this attempted freeing move is premature, as the open lines benefit only White.

6 dxe5 ♕a5+ 7 ♗d2 ♕xe5 8 0-0-0 ♘xe4

Or 8...♕xe4 9 ♖e1 pinning and winning the queen.

9 ♕d8+!! ♔xd8 10 ♗g5++

Discovering a check from the rook on d1 as well, so we have discovered attack and double check.

10...♔c7

10...♔e8 11 ♖d8 #.

11 ♗d8 #

The 'smothered mate' combination depends on a double check:

Timman-Short
Tilburg 1990

1 ♕c4+! ♔h8 2 ♘f7+ ♔g8 3 ♘h6++

Double check, from queen and knight.

3...♔h8 4 ♕g8+! ♖xg8 5 ♘f7#

The black king is smothered by his own defenders.

Morphy v NN
1859

1 ♘c5+ ♔b8 2 ♘d7+ ♔c8 3 ♘b6++

A second discovered check.

3...♔b8 4 ♕c8+ ♖xc8 5 ♘d7#

3   The Endgame

Introduction

A chess game can usually be divided into three phases: opening, middlegame and endgame. Not every game has all three, though; a decision may be reached (or a draw agreed!) in the opening or middlegame, while sometimes an endgame will arise straight out of the opening.

Endgame specialist GM Edmar Mednis wrote a particularly good book entitled *From the Opening into the Endgame* designed to show tournament players how to reach favourable endings from certain openings. At a tournament in the US, Mednis was seen to suffer a swift defeat, which led one GM to comment 'From the Opening into the Pub'. As Siegbert Tarrasch said, 'before the endgame the gods have placed the opening and the middlegame'.

The opening is the initial phase of the game, in which the players' main task is to get their pieces off the back rank and into play. The endgame begins when most of the pieces have been exchanged, the danger of checkmate recedes, and the battle to promote a pawn takes centre stage. The middlegame is everything that happens in between! In practice, a game rarely divides neatly into categories, and so our 'definitions' are left intentionally vague.

The endgame is a time when accuracy is at a premium. In the opening or middlegame, there may be a variety of attractive moves to choose from, but in the endgame the second best move may well be a losing blunder!

Knowledge of simple endgames is essential and I won't disguise the fact there is some good old-fashioned memory work required here. The king and pawn endgames are essential, as are elementary checkmates.

Elementary Checkmates

♔+♕ v ♚

This is entirely straightforward: the weaker side's king is driven to the edge of the board and checkmated. The only pitfall is accidentally giving stalemate − so if your opponent's king is trapped on the edge with your queen a knight's move away, make sure you leave him an escape square!

1 ♔b7 ♔e4 2 ♔c6 ♔f5 3 ♔d5 ♔f4
4 ♕c3 ♔f5 5 ♕f3+ ♔g5 6 ♔e6 ♔g6
7 ♕g4+ ♔h6 8 ♔f7 ♔h7 9 ♕g7#

♔+♖ v ♔

Once again, the weaker side's king must be driven to the edge. Watch out for the rook's waiting move one before the end. This is an example of *Zugzwang* – a German word which roughly translates as 'compulsion to move'. *Zugzwang*, occasionally referred to jokingly as 'Volkswagen', is the name given to a situation where the player to move would have a satisfactory game, if only he could pass the move to his opponent; as it is, he must move, and whatever he plays will ruin his position. *Zugzwang* occurs remarkably often in the endgame.

1 ♔b7 ♔e4 2 ♔c6
The rook can't mate on its own; the king must be brought in first.
2...♔d4 3 ♖e1
As in queen v king, the extra piece is used to cut off the defending king.
3...♔c4 4 ♖e4+ ♔d3 5 ♔d5 ♔c3
6 ♖d4

The king is now confined to a 3x3 square box.
6...♔c2 7 ♔c4 ♔b2 8 ♖d2+ ♔c1
9 ♔c3 ♔b1 10 ♔b3 ♔c1 11 ♖d3!
This cunning waiting move is the essential point to remember in this endgame. Now the black king is forced to walk into a mate in one.
11...♔b1 12 ♖d1#

♔+♗+♗ v ♔

The two bishops occupy adjacent diagonals and drive the enemy king to a corner, supported as ever by their own king.

1 ♔b2 ♔e4 2 ♔c3 ♔d5 3 ♗f3+
♔e5 4 ♗g3+ ♔e6 5 ♔d4 ♔f5 6
♔d5 ♔f6 7 ♗g4 ♔g5 8 ♗d7 ♔f6
9 ♗h4+ ♔g6 10 ♔e5 ♔f7 11 ♔f5
♔g7 12 ♗e8 ♔f8 13 ♗g6 ♔g7 14
♗e7 ♔g8

14...♔h6 15 ♗f8#.
15 ♔f6 ♔h8 16 ♗f5 ♔g8 17 ♔g6
♔h8 18 ♗d6
Another waiting move. 18 ♗f6+
♔g8 19 ♗e6+ ♔f8 would delay matters.
18...♔g8 19 ♗e6+ ♔h8 20 ♗e5#

♚+♗+♘ *v* ♚

This is the trickiest of the mates in this section. The weaker side's king can only be mated in a corner of the colour controlled by the bishop. The safest method is first to drive the king to an edge, and then chase him along it towards the correct corner.

1 ♔b2 ♚d3 2 ♘c7 ♚c4 3 ♘e6 ♚d5 4 ♘d4 ♚c4 5 ♔c2 ♚b4 6 ♔d3 ♚c5 7 ♗h2 ♚d5 8 ♘b3 ♚c6 9 ♔c4 ♚b6 10 ♘c5 ♚c6 11 ♘a4 ♚b7 12 ♔b5 ♚c8 13 ♔c6 ♚d8 14 ♔d6 ♚c8 15 ♘b6+ ♚b7 16 ♔c5 ♚a6 17 ♔c6 ♚a5 18 ♗d6 ♚a6 19 ♗b8 ♚a5 20 ♘d5 ♚a4

Or 20...♚a6 21 ♘b4+ ♚a5 22 ♔c5 ♚a4 23 ♔c4 ♚a5 24 ♗c7+.

21 ♔c5 ♚b3 22 ♘b4 ♚c3 23 ♗f4 ♚b3 24 ♗e5 ♚a4 25 ♔c4 ♚a5 26 ♗c7+ ♚a4 27 ♘d3 ♚a3 28 ♗b6 ♚a4 29 ♘b2+ ♚a3 30 ♔c3 ♚a2 31 ♔c2 ♚a3 32 ♗c5+ ♚a2 33 ♘d3 ♚a1 34 ♗b4 ♚a2 35 ♘c1+ ♚a1 36 ♗c3#

♚+♘+♘ *v* ♚

This is a draw, unless the weaker side is extremely co-operative!

We start with the black king already in the corner. Try playing around from the starting position; there are all sorts of ways to stalemate but none to *force* checkmate. All the defender need do is avoid mates in one. For example:

1 ♘f8 ♚g8 2 ♘d7 ♚h8 3 ♘d6 ♚g8 4 ♘f6+ and now 4...♚f8

Not 4...♚h8?? 5 ♘f7#.

Other Pawnless Endings

A general rule is that an advantage of four 'points' is usually necessary and sufficient to win. It follows that ♕v♖ is a win, but ♖v♘, ♖v♗, ♕+♘v♕, ♕+♗v♕, ♕v♘+♘, ♖+♘v♖ and ♖+♗v♖ are normally drawn. There are positions in all these endings which contradict this rule, and ♖+♗v♖ in particular is notoriously treacherous for the defender.

Further exceptions to the rule are the extremely rare, but generally winning, endings of ♗+♗v♘, ♕v♗+♗ and ♕v♗+♘.

All five-piece endgames with no more than one pawn have been analysed out and put on CD. This gargantuan work was performed by Professor Ken Thompson, the developer of the UNIX computer operating system. During this analysis the anomalies referred to in the discussion of the 50 move rule were discovered. Endgame fanatics can purchase a complete collection of these CDs for about £100 ($150).

♕ *v* ♖

With White to move, the plan is to lose a move and reach the same position with Black to play – putting him in zugzwang. In practice this endgame is always won very quickly but in theory it requires great accuracy. I recall with amusement an afternoon at the Chess Olympiad in Thessaloniki in 1988. Frederic Friedel and Matthias Wüllenweber of the chess database company ChessBase GmbH in Hamburg brought a disk with a complete analysis of this endgame. The computer knew exactly how to respond in every position to make the win as difficult as possible and a display above the board showed how far off the win was. Former world champion Boris Spassky and leading GM Alexander Beliavsky sweated over it for three hours before winning with the queen. They would make a move and the computer would say 'win 10 moves away', then 9, then 8 – then they would make a mistake and back went the display to 15 moves to win. Don't worry; in practice the player with the rook always loses quickly.

Philidor

Black to move is in zugzwang: wherever the rook goes, it will be exposed to a lethal fork:

1...♖b3 2 ♕d8+ ♔a7 3 ♕d4+ ♔b8 4 ♕f4+ ♔a7 5 ♕a4+.

1...♖f7 2 ♕e5+ ♔a7 3 ♕e3+ ♔b8 4 ♕e8+.

1...♖h7 2 ♕e5+ ♔a7 3 ♕a1+ ♔b8 4 ♕b1+.

1...♔c8 2 ♕a6.

1...♖b1 2 ♕d8+ ♔a7 3 ♕d4+ ♔a8 4 ♕h8+ ♔a7 5 ♕h7+.

White to play can lose a move by triangulating with his queen:

1 ♕e5+ ♔a8 2 ♕a1+ ♔b8 3 ♕a5

Now we have the starting position with Black to move and he is again in zugzwang.

It may seem strange to see players so keen to *lose* a move in the endgame, but there is a good reason for this. Zugzwang arises when the player to move already has every unit on its best square; such efficiency is more likely the fewer the pieces that remain.

The endgames of rook v bishop and rook v knight are generally drawn with best play although there are some exceptions. Rook and knight v rook is relatively easy to defend and is a theoretical draw, but rook and bishop v rook is frequently lost in practice although with a few exceptions it should be drawn.

Pawn Endings

♚+♙ v ♚

The result of this endgame often depends on who has 'the Opposition'. When the kings stand in line, separated by an odd number of squares, the player who is *not* to move is said to have the Opposition – the reason this is so important is that it means the enemy king has to give way.

White has just played ♚e4, placing one square between himself and the enemy king, thus taking the Opposition.

Here, Black to play loses: **1...♚d8 2 d7 ♚c7 3 ♚e7**.

The weaker side has more resources against an h-pawn: in this case, the Opposition no longer matters, as there is a stalemate defence. The weaker side draws if his king is inside the pawn's Square and has access to f8.

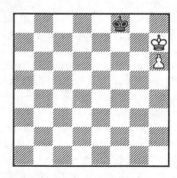

1 ♚g6 ♚g8 2 h7+ ♚h8
The position is drawn.

Now a difficult example to see how much you have learned.

Fischer-Gligoric
Yugoslavia Ct 1959

White played **1 ♔c4**. How do you keep the opposition?

1...♚b8!

A draw was agreed here, as Black takes the 'distant opposition'. Other moves lose, e.g. 1...♚c7?? 1 ♔c5 or 1...♚d7?? 2 ♔d5.

A possible continuation is **2 ♔c5 ♚c7 3 ♔b5 ♚b7**, and White cannot improve his position.

The Rule of the Square

This is essentially a short cut for calculating the race between a passed pawn and a king trying to intercept the pawn on its way to the queening square. First count the number of moves a pawn must make to reach its queening square, then count the same number of squares along the rank towards the king. These two sides mark out the Square in question, and the Rule is simple: the king can catch the pawn if and only if he can move into its Square.

In the following diagram the white king to move can catch the black pawn but the black king to move cannot catch the white pawn.

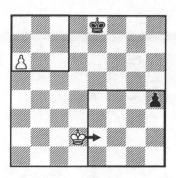

Passed Pawns

Passed pawns are one of the most important features in any endgame, and an awful lot of effort is expended in trying to create and then advance them.

A passed pawn is a pawn whose path to its queening square is unobstructed by enemy pawns.

An outside passed pawn is a passed pawn distant from the main field of action.

A protected passed pawn is a passed pawn defended by another pawn. This is particularly potent because it ties down enemy pieces because of its threat to advance.

A pawn majority is a greater number of pawns than the opponent on one side of the board.

In the next example White has a 3-2 majority on the kingside, while Black has a 3-2 majority on the queenside. However, Black's pawn majority includes a doubled pawn and is rendered useless, as it is unable to create a passed pawn, and so White has a 'qualitative majority' on the queenside − leaving him to all intents and purposes a whole pawn up. He wins as follows:

1 ♔e4

1...b5 2 f4 a5 3 g4 b4 4 f5+ ♔f6 5 h4 h6 6 ♔f4 a4 7 b3 b5 8 g5+ hxg5+ 9 hxg5+ ♔e7 10 ♔e5 ♔f7 11 ♔d5 ♔e7 12 ♔c5 and White takes the black queenside pawns.

Zugzwang again plays a critical role in pawn endings. In the following position, whoever moves loses! This is an example of reciprocal (or mutual) zugzwang.

We will take White to move. Whatever he tries, he is the first to run out of pawn moves and must give way with his king, so long as Black copies everything he does.

1 a3 a6

Not **1...a5?? 2 a4 b6 3 b3** when White wins.

2 b3 b6 3 b4 b5 and Black wins.

This example illustrates another important rule for pawn endings: keep as many pawn moves in reserve as you can – they are priceless in the battle to lose a move!

Creating a passed pawn
Here is a basic example

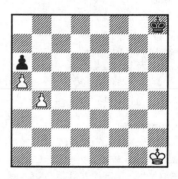

1 b5 axb5 2 a6 and promotes to a new queen.

The breakthrough

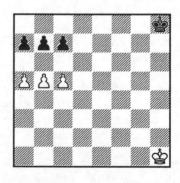

White to play wins with **1 b6 axb6 2 c6 bxc6 3 a6.**

The passed pawn is the most potent weapon in the endgame

Outside Passed Pawn

This is often a deciding factor in any endgame because it deflects enemy pieces trying to prevent its advance. In the following example Black has an extra pawn but the outside passed pawn is decisive.

The white passed pawn is on the outside and this is decisive.

1 ♔d3 ♔b3

1...♔c5 2 b4+ ♔d5 3 b5 ♔c5 4 b6 ♔xb6 5 ♔xd4 ♔c6 6 ♔e5.

2 ♔xd4 ♔xb2 3 ♔e5 ♔c3 4 ♔f6 ♔d4 5 ♔xg6 ♔e5 6 ♔xh5 and White wins.

A famous study by Réti:

White seems utterly lost: Black's h-pawn is on the rampage, while his last foot-soldier is going nowhere fast. What follows is a miracle of geometry.

1 ♔g7 h4 2 ♔f6 ♔b6

2...h3 3 ♔e7 h2 4 c7 h1♕ (4...♔b7 5 ♔d7 is no better) 5 c8♕+ ♕b7+.

3 ♔e5! h3

3...♔xc6 4 ♔f4 h3 5 ♔g3.

4 ♔d6 h2 5 c7 h1♕ 6 c8♕ and White draws. Who said the shortest distance between two points was a straight line?

Queen Endings

♕ *v* ♟

This might sound like a mismatch, but when the pawn is just one step short of queening it can put up a real fight! The stronger side must check the enemy king in front of his pawn, and then use his moment's respite to bring his own king closer, as below:

White must force the black king to e1, where it obstructs the pawn; this buys him a move to advance his own king.

1 ♕f7+ ♔g2 2 ♕g6+ ♔f2 3 ♕f5+ ♔g2 4 ♕e4+ ♔f2 5 ♕f4+ ♔g2 6 ♕e3 ♔f1 7 ♕f3+ ♔e1 8 ♔c5 ♔d2

Now the same process is repeated, until White's king is near enough to weave a mating net.

9 ♕f2 ♔d1 10 ♕d4+ ♔c1 11 ♕e3+ ♔d1 12 ♕d3+ ♔e1 13 ♔d4 ♔f2 14 ♕e3+ ♔f1 15 ♕f3+ ♔e1 16 ♔d3 ♔d1 17 ♕xe2+ ♔c1 18 ♕c2#

This method wins against a b- or d-pawn in all but a few exceptional circumstances (i.e. when the queen is prevented from giving check or pinning the pawn by her own king's position). A c- or a-pawn improves the defender's chances, as he has a stalemate defence. Only if his king is close enough to support a checkmate can the superior side win these positions.

In this case, White's king is close enough to force a win.

1 ♕d4+ ♔b1 2 ♕d1+ ♔b2 3 ♕d2+ ♔b1 4 ♔c4! a1♕
4...a1♘ 5 ♔c3.
5 ♔b3!
This fearless king advance leaves Black with no sensible checks, and forces checkmate shortly.

1 ♕a2 ♔d1 2 ♕a4 ♔d2 3 ♕d4+ ♔e2 4 ♕c3 ♔d1 5 ♕d3+ ♔c1 6 ♔b7 ♔b2

The black king heads for the corner, with a stalemate defence in mind.

7 ♕d2 ♔b1 8 ♕b4+ ♔a2 9 ♕c3 ♔b1 10 ♕b3+ ♔a1!

This is the point: the threat to capture on c2 is empty, but White has no constructive alternative.

11 ♕xc2
Stalemate.

♕ *v* ♕, *numerous pawns*

The most important factors here are passed pawns and king safety – unusually, the number of pawns on each side is less important. An active, centralised queen is also a big plus. As in all endings with pieces, you must always keep a look-out for possible transpositions into a king and pawn ending.

Pein-de Firmian
Bermuda 1995

This is taken from one of my own games, against Nick de Firmian, the Californian GM who was rated in the world's top 100 at the time. The tournament was the Mermaid Beach International at the Mermaid Beach Club on Bermuda, an idyllic setting for a chess tournament and one of David Norwood's favourite hangouts – indeed he also played. Readers of the *DT* chess may recall the episode reported in my column where Norwood threatened to jump into the sea if he lost any more games. In fact apart from a shock defeat at my hands Dave had a pretty good tournament while I was delighted to score 50% in such exalted company. This example illustrates quite well the points about king safety and passed pawns. I am White, and I am winning. Not only do I have an extra pawn but my king is totally safe while my pawns advance with gain of time because of the threats they create against Nick's king. The first step is to protect the f2-pawn and put my king on the same diagonal as my queen thus preventing any annoying checks.

46 ♔g2 a5

Black's only chance is to push his passed pawn as fast as possible but the weakness of the black king costs several tempi in the race.

47 ♕d7+ ♔g8

If 47...♔g6, 48 h5+! ♔xh5 49 ♕h7+ ♔g4 50 ♕h4#. So I win a pawn.

48 ♕xf5 a4 49 ♕g6+

An important move as it forces the win of the f6-pawn with check.

49...♔f8 50 ♕xf6+ ♔e8 51 ♕e5+

The queen is at its most powerful in the centre. I reach this square, from where my queen defends the

black pawn's queening square a1 and my pawn's square on h8, with gain of time.

51...♔f7 52 h5 a3 53 h6 ♕b2 54 h7

This leads to ♕+2 pawns v ♕ but I could have had ♕+3 v ♕! The key line was 54 ♕d5+ ♔e7 (54...♔g6 55 ♕g5+ ♔h7 56 f5 a2 57 ♕g6+ ♔h8 58 ♕e8+ ♔h7 59 ♕f7+ ♔h8 60 f6 mates) 55 h7 a2 56 ♕e5+ ♕xe5 57 fxe5 a1♕ 58 h8♕ – then even I would have had a problem messing it up.

54...♕xe5 55 fxe5 ♔g7 56 e6 a2 57 e7 a1♕ 58 e8♕ ♔xh7

This is a simple technical win but in the quickplay finish I contrived to draw.

59 g4 ♕d1 60 ♕e4+ ♔h8 61 g5 ♔g7 62 ♕e5+ ♔h7 63 ♕f5+ ♔g7 64 ♕f6+ ♔g8 65 g6??

Everyone in the room from spectator to GM had seen what was coming apart from me.

65...♕g4+ 66 ♔h2

Nick's arm reached out, I thought he was resigning but he was reaching for g2, not my sweaty palm.

66...♕g2+ ½-½

This example also illustrates Tartakower's maxim 'Sit on the hands when the win is in sight'.

Rook Endings

The Lucena Position

If the king reaches the queening square the game is usually won. First of all, White must drive the enemy king from the e-file.

1 ℤe1+ ♔d7

White wins more quickly after 1...♔f6 2 ♔f8 since the black king shields the white king from checks, or 1...♔d6 2 ♔f8 ℤf2+ 3 ♔e8 ℤg2 4 ℤe7 ℤg1 5 ♔f8 ℤf1+ 6 ℤf7.

2 ℤe4!

White's plan is to extricate his king from the pawn's queening square, using the rook to shield it from checks. This manoeuvre is called 'building a bridge'.

2...ℤh1 3 ♔f7 ℤf1+ 4 ♔g6 ℤg1+ 5 ♔f6 ℤf1+ 6 ♔g5 ℤg1+ 7 ℤg4

The bridge is complete, and the pawn queens – but only because the preliminary check drove the black king from e7.

Philidor's Draw

This study by Philidor is actually an exception to the rule about putting your rook behind a passed pawn. If 1...ℤe1 2 ♔e6 followed by ℤh8+ driving the black king away from the queening square.

1...ℤa6!

Black must stop the king advancing.

2 ℤb7 ℤc6

Waiting.

3 ℤa7 ℤb6 4 e6

Given that the rook has no inclination to desert the third rank, this advance is the only serious attempt to make progress. However, this allows Black to change plans and force a draw.

4...♖b1!

Taking advantage of the fact that the white king can no longer shelter from checks from the rear.

5 ♔f6 ♖f1+ 6 ♔e5 ♖e1+ 7 ♔d6 ♖d1+

If the king heads for the eighth rank, and the protection of its rook, simply ...♖e1 collects the e-pawn.

More pawns

Rook endings are the most common, and arguably the most difficult, kind of endgame. Even very strong GMs regularly mess them up, so much so that an old Russian proverb goes 'All rook endings are drawn'. The golden rule is to play actively: an active king and rook are usually worth an extra pawn. The rook is usually most active *behind* a passed pawn, either friendly or hostile, so that its power increases every time the pawn steps forward.

Spielmann-Rubinstein
St Petersburg 1909

Black has a better pawn structure, because White has four isolated pawns but this is compensated for by the passed a-pawn. Such a pawn is known as an outside passed pawn: passed and on the opposite side of the board to the kings. In the king and pawn endgame an outside passed pawn is often decisive because the time taken to stop and then capture it often allows the opponent's king a free hand elsewhere.

1...♖a8

1...♖b3 2 ♖a2 ♖d3 3 a4 ♖xd4 4 a5 ♖c4 5 a6 ♖c8 6 a7 ♖a8 7 ♔g3 ♔e7 8 ♔f4 ♔d7 9 ♔e4 ♔c6 10 ♔d4 holds out no hope of a win for Black, as any attempt to round up the a-pawn results in a lost ♔+♙ endgame.

2 ♖c3?!

2 ♖a2 ('rooks behind passed pawns!') 2...♖a4 3 ♔g3! is probably White's saving grace: ...♖xd4 allows the a-pawn too much activity, as before.

2...♖a4! 3 ♖d3

Now the white rook is extremely passive, tied down to the defence of two weak pawns.

3...♔e7 4 ♔g3 ♔e6 5 ♔f3 ♔d5 6 ♔e2!?

This is the position White had been aiming for: 6...♖xd4?? 7 ♔e3! ♖xd3+ 8 ♔xd3 gives him a won ending, thanks to the outside passed a-pawn.

6...g5!

6...♖xd4 7 ♔e3 ♖xd3+ 8 ♔xd3.

7 ♖b3 f6

Rubinstein spurns the pawn again, since 7...♔xd4 allows 8 ♖b7 with counterplay.

8 ♔e3 ♔c4 9 ♖d3 d5 10 ♔d2 ♖a8 11 ♔c2 ♖a7! 12 ♔d2 ♖e7!

Thanks to the preparatory waiting move (11...♖a7!), White now finds himself in zugzwang. 13 ♔c2 ♖e2+ 14 ♖d2 ♖xd2+ 15 ♔xd2 ♔b3! is completely hopeless.

13 ♖c3+

13 ♖e3 ♖b7 14 ♖d3 ♖b2+ 15 ♔e3 ♖xf2!.

13...♔xd4 14 a4 ♖a7 15 ♖a3 ♖a5

Rubinstein's patience has been rewarded. He has won a pawn without relaxing his grip on the position, and now blockades the a-pawn before embarking on any further active operations.

16 ♖a1 ♔c4

17 ♔e3?!

Spielmann's last chance was to sacrifice a second pawn for some activity with 17 ♖c1+ ♔b4 18 ♖b1+ ♔xa4 19 ♔d3 ♖c5 (19...♖b5? 20 ♖a1+ ♔b4 21 ♔d4 might even lose for Black) 20 ♔d4 ♖c2 21 ♖b7 ♖xc2 22 ♖xg7.

17...d4+ 18 ♔d2 ♖f5! 19 ♔e1

19 a5 ♖xf2+ 20 ♔e1 ♖b2 21 a6 ♖b8 22 a7 ♖a8 23 ♔d2 ♔c5 24 ♔d3 ♔b6 25 ♔xd4 ♖xa7 is a win for Black.

19...♔b4 20 ♔e2 ♔a5!

Changing the guard at a5, so that the rook is free to attack White's pawns.

21 ♖a3 ♖f4 22 ♖a2 ♖h4 23 ♔d3 ♖xh3+ 24 ♔xd4 ♖h4+ 25 ♔d3

♖xa4 26 ♖e2 ♖f4 27 ♔e3 ♔b6 28 ♖c2 ♔b7 29 ♖c1 ♖a4 30 ♖h1 ♔c6 31 ♖h7 ♖a7 32 ♔e4 ♔d6 33 ♔f5 g6+! 34 ♔xg6 ♖xh7 35 ♔xh7 ♔e5 36 ♔g6 g4 0-1

Rubinstein's mastery of rook endings is legendary, and this classic shows the value of not hurrying to convert an endgame advantage, but keeping control of the position at all times.

Bishop Endings

These fall into two categories, according to whether the bishops move on squares of the same or opposite colour.

Same-colour bishops

♗+♙ *v* ♗

The weaker side draws easily if his king gets in front of the pawn, to a square of the opposite colour to the bishops. However, if the stronger side's king gets there first, he stands to win – Centurini's position below is a beautiful illustration of the technique required.

Centurini, 1847

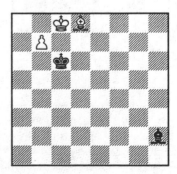

White's task is to drive the black bishop from the h2-b8 diagonal; therefore he must find a way to manoeuvre his bishop round to b8.

1 ♗h4 ♔b5 2 ♗f2 ♔a6 3 ♗c5!

This is the key move: it is essential to prevent 3...♗d6, for reasons which soon become apparent.

3...♗g3

3...♔b5 4 ♗a7.

4 ♗e7 ♔b5 5 ♗d8 ♔c6

The only change from the initial position is that Black's bishop has moved one square up the diagonal – but this is all White needs!

6 ♗h4!

If Black had played 3...♗f4 or 3...♗e5, the move here would be 6 ♗g5! or 6 ♗f6! accordingly.

6...♗h2 7 ♗f2

Now we see why 3...♗d6 had to be prevented: after 6 ♗e7 ♗h2, White would be unable to transfer his bishop to the g1-a7 diagonal.

7...♗f4 8 ♗a7 ♗h2 9 ♗b8 ♗g1 10 ♗g3 ♗a7 11 ♗f2!

Black's bishop has been chased to the shortest diagonal, and has nowhere left to hide. Black's bishop has been chased to the shortest diagonal, and has nowhere left to hide.

With more pawns, the question of 'good' and 'bad' bishops may arise. A bishop is 'bad' if it is obstructed by its own pawns (especially central pawns) fixed on squares of the colour it controls. This may appear odd at first sight; pawns on the same colour as one's bishop can be protected easily but they are also vulnerable to attack from the enemy bishop. Good v bad bishop positions usually give good winning chances to the superior side.

Pein-Popchev
Val Thorens 1990

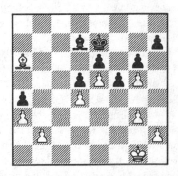

This is from my game against the Bulgarian International Master Milko Popchev from the Val Thorens tournament at the famous Olympic skiing resort high in the French Alps. The pawns seemed to go faster at altitude. Although I have an extra pawn the win is far from easy but Black's bishop is very bad and by playing on both wings I won as follows.

35...⌨d8 36 ⌨f2

The first step in most endgames is to activate the king which is a very strong piece once queens have been exchanged and the threat of mate recedes.

36...⌨c7 37 ⌨e3 ⌨b6 38 ♝d3 ♝e8 39 ♝e2 ⌨a5 40 ♝d1 ♝b5 41 ♝e2 ♝e8

41...♝xe2 is met by 42 ⌨xe2 followed by ⌨d2-c3 and b3 creating an outside passed pawn.

42 g4

A typical feature of bad bishop endings is the vulnerability of the defender to an attack on two points simultaneously. Because of a lack of space caused by being hemmed in by its own pawns the defending bishop often only has one square from where it defends two points simultaneously so he can often fall into zugzwang.

42...fxg4 43 ♝xg4 ♝f7 44 h4 ⌨b6 45 ♝d1 ⌨b5 46 ♝e2+ ⌨a5 47 ♝d3 ♝e8 48 h5 ♝f7

48...gxh5 49 ♝xh7 and g6.

49 hxg6 hxg6

Now the black bishop is tied to the g6-pawn and can defend that and the a4-square only from e8. Black needs to guard a4 to prevent the advance of my passed pawn after I play b3; zugzwang approaches.

50 ⌨d2 ♝e8 51 ⌨c3 ♝f7 52 b3 axb3 53 ⌨xb3 ♝e8 54 ♝c2

I lose a move.

54...⌨b5 55 a4+ ⌨a5 56 ⌨a3 ♝f7

56...⌨b6 57 ⌨b4 makes more progress.

57 ♝b1 ♝e8 58 ♝d3 1-0

Black is in zugzwang. After 58...♝f7, 59 ♝b5 ♝g8 60 ♝e8 ♝h7

61 ♝f7 makes the bishop not bad but non-existent.

Opposite-colour bishops

These endings have a strong tendency towards a draw, as the weaker side can often neutralise a disadvantage of one or even two pawns by setting up a blockade on whichever colour squares he controls. In contrast to same colour bishop endings, the weaker side should place his pawns on the *same* colour squares as his bishop controls, where they will be safe from the enemy bishop. Normally a material *and* positional advantage is necessary to force a win, such as an extra outside passed pawn, or two widely separated passed pawns.

This diagram illustrates a typical blockade. White is two pawns up, but if Black's bishop maintains a watch on the e5-square, White can make no progress.

Bishop and wrong-colour rook's pawn

A rook's (i.e. a- or h-) pawn is of the 'wrong' colour if its queening square is of the colour not controlled by the bishop. In this case, the weaker side draws if his king gets to the corner in time, as there is nothing in the world that can winkle him out!

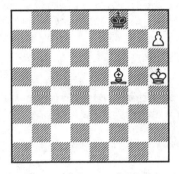

1...♔g7

The position is dead drawn. Very frustrating, isn't it?

Knight Endings

Knight endings resemble pawn endings in that an extra pawn usually wins. The threat of exchanging knights into a won king and pawn endgame can be used to great effect. The knight's short hops are badly-suited to dealing with enemy passed pawns, and two well-separated passed pawns supported by a king will often beat a knight – a typical winning method is for the superior side to sacrifice his knight for a pawn or two to reach such a situation. A rook's pawn is especially trouble-some, since the knight is much weaker at the edge of the board and can only attack a rook's pawn from one side.

Vasiukov-Timoshchenko
Volgodonsk 1981

White's dominant king gives him an obvious advantage, but the win requires some fine technique.

1 ♘e4 ♔e8 2 ♔d6

2 ♘xg5 ♘f2 would have given Black every chance of a draw.

2...♔f8 3 ♘xc5 ♘f2 4 ♘d7+ ♔f7 5 ♘e5+

So White has grabbed a pawn without compromising his position. However, he must avoid committing his king to the queenside, as this could allow Black to sacrifice his knight for the c-pawn and mop up the g-pawn with his king.

5...♔f6 6 ♔d5 ♘d1 7 c5 ♘c3+ 8 ♔c4 ♘e4 9 ♘d3 ♔e6 10 ♔d4 ♘f6 11 ♘f2 ♔e7 12 c6 ♔e6

12...♔d6? 13 ♘e4+ loses without a fight.

13 ♔c5 ♔e7 14 ♔b6 ♔d6 15 ♘h3!

The knight must ignore the g-pawn, on pain of allowing the c-pawn through to queen.

15...♘d5+ 16 ♔b7 ♔e5 17 ♘xg5 ♔f4 18 ♘h7!

The g-pawn is leading a charmed life – now 18...♔xg4 fails to 19 ♘f6+ ♘xf6 20 c7 and 21 c8♕(+).

18...♘c3 19 g5

There was still a chance to go wrong with 19 c7?? ♘b5 20 c8♕ ♘d6+ etc.

19...♔f5 20 c7 1-0

But now on 20...♘b5, White queens with check.

Alekhine-Andersen
Folkestone OL 1933

1 ♘b3!

White has the more active knight and his king is already near the centre. Alekhine uses this to force the win of the a7-pawn for his d5-pawn; he then has an outside passed pawn.

1...♔f8

1...♘e7 2 ♘a5 ♘xd5 3 ♘xb7 ♘f4 4 ♘xd6 ♘d3+ 5 ♔c2 ♘xf2 6 b4 ♔f8 7 a4 ♘g4 (7...♔e7 8 ♘c8+) 8 b5 ♘xh2 9 a5 ♔e7 10 b6 axb6 11 a6 is a trick worth remembering.

2 ♘a5 b6 3 ♘c6 ♔e8 4 ♔d2 ♘e7 5 ♘xa7 ♘xd5 6 ♘b5 ♔d7 7 ♘d4 g6 8 a4 ♘c7 9 ♔c3 g5 10 ♔b4 d5 11 ♘f3 f6 12 ♘d4 ♔d6

12...♔e7 13 a5 bxa5+ 14 ♔xa5 ♔d7 15 b4 ♔c8 16 ♔b6.

13 ♘b5+ ♘xb5 14 ♔xb5 ♔e5 15 b4 d4 16 ♔c4 1-0

The outside passed pawn decides matters.

Bishop v Knight Endings

According to the 'points' scale in Chapter 2, the bishop and knight are of equal value. This may (or may not!) be true over a very large sample of games, but there are many situations in which one is clearly stronger than the other.

The bishop is stronger when...
 ♗ the pawn position is open
 ♗ there is play on both sides of the board
 ♗ rooks are present

The knight is stronger when...
 ♘ the pawn position is blocked
 ♘ there is play on only one side the board
 ♘ queens are present

♖+♗ v ♖+♘: *Fischer's Endgame*

Fischer-Taimanov
Vancouver Ct (4) 1971

The vast majority of players would regard White's advantage here as, at best, minimal. In fact, Fischer's superior minor piece, more active rook and better pawn structure all add up, and his flawless technique does the rest. Such was Fischer's ability in this type of position that it became known as the Fischer endgame.

1 ♗f1 a5 2 ♗c4 ♖f8

In two simple moves, Fischer forces another weakening pawn move, and ties the black rook to the defence of f7. Now he must improve the position of his king before committing himself to a specific plan.

3 ♔g2 ♔d6 4 ♔f3 ♘d7 5 ♖e3 ♘b8 6 ♖d3+ ♔c7 7 c3

This move deprives the knight of the potential outposts at d4 and b4, preventing it from playing an active role in the game.

7...♘c6 8 ♖e3 ♔d6 9 a4

This is an important move, fixing the queenside weaknesses in place.

9...♘e7 10 h3 ♘c6 11 h4 h5

This holds up Fischer's intended space-gaining advance, but leaves Black's kingside pawns fixed on light squares.

12 ♖d3+ ♔c7 13 ♖d5 f5 14 ♖d2 ♖f6 15 ♖e2 ♔d7 16 ♖e3 g6

Black's pawns have become fixed on the same colour square as White's bishop.

17 ♗b5 ♖d6 18 ♔e2 ♔d8 19 ♖d3!

Fischer forces the exchange of rooks, confident of winning the minor piece ending that follows. The bishop will tie the knight to the defence of g6, clearing the way for the king to penetrate to a6.

19...♔c7 20 ♖xd6 ♔xd6 21 ♔d3 ♘e7 22 ♗e8 ♔d5 23 ♗f7+ ♔d6 24

♔c4 ♔c6 25 ♗e8+ ♔b7 26 ♔b5 ♘c8 27 ♗c6+

Premature is 27 ♗xg6?? ♘d6#.

27...♔c7 28 ♗d5 ♘e7 29 ♗f7 ♔b7

Fischer must now drive the black king from b7, which means transferring the bishop to the long diagonal.

30 ♗b3 ♔a7 31 ♗d1 ♔b7 32 ♗f3+ ♔c7

32...♔a7 33 c4 places Black in zugzwang, as a knight move allows the white king to invade the kingside via c6.

33 ♔a6 ♘g8 34 ♗d5 ♘e7

34...♘f6 35 ♗f7 ♘e4 36 ♗xg6 ♘xg3 37 c4 ♔c6 38 ♔a7 ♔c7 39 ♗f7 ♘e2 40 ♗xh5 ♘xf4 41 ♗f7 wins for White, as the knight is no match for his h-pawn.

35 ♗c4 ♘c6 36 ♗f7 ♘e7 37 ♗e8

This is the position Fischer had foreseen around twenty moves previously; Black is in zugzwang.

37...♔d8 38 ♗xg6!!

The point: Black's uncoordinated pieces cannot fend off the 'space invaders' on the queenside.

38...♘xg6 39 ♔xb6 ♔d7 40 ♔xc5 ♘e7 41 b4 axb4 42 cxb4 ♘c8 43 a5

♘d6 44 b5 ♘e4+ 45 ♔b6 ♔c8 46 ♔c6 ♔b8 47 b6 1-0

Since the white king now goes to the kingside.

Good knight v Bad bishop

Pein-Stepak
Ramat Hasharon 1990

This is from a game of mine against the Israeli Master Yedael Stepak. White has a completely won position because of the superiority of the knight over the bad bishop. The knight protects my position and has a lot of inviting targets such as a5 or c7. Note that a bad bishop hemmed in by pawns of its own colour cannot attack enemy pawns since they are going to be fixed on the opposite-coloured square. To win all I have to do is penetrate with my king.

40 ♔f3 ♗e7 41 ♔e3 ♔g6 42 g4

Note how a light-squared knight, which attacks dark squares, and a light-squared pawn, which covers light squares, combine to form an impenetrable barrier.

42...hxg4 43 hxg4 ♔f7 44 ♔d3 ♔e8 45 c5

A breakthrough sacrifice allows the king to march in via c4.

45...dxc5 46 ♔c4 ♔d7 47 ♘xc5+ ♔c8

After 47...♗xc5 48 ♔xc5 g6 49 g5 ♔e7 50 ♔c6 ♔d8 51 d6 cxd6 52 ♔xd6 White wins the e5-pawn.

48 ♘b3 ♗h4 49 f3 a4 50 ♘c5 a3 51 b3

Now all Black's pawns drop off.

51...♗e7 52 ♘d3 ♗d6 53 ♘xb4 ♔b7 54 ♘c2 c6 55 dxc6+ ♔xc6 56 b4 1-0

Stalemate

Chernin-Dunnington
Cappelle la Grande 1994

42 ♕f6??

White is winning easily, but relaxes too soon and allows his opponent to save himself. The careful 42 ♕e5 would have sufficed.

42...h4+! 43 ♔xh4 ♖b8!!

A stunning resource: suddenly Black is playing for stalemate.

44 ♖xb8

White must acquiesce, as he is certainly not better after 44 ♖a6 ♕xd5.

44...♕xh3+! 45 ♔xh3 ½-½

4   The Middlegame

Strategy in the Middlegame

King Safety

Technical endgames are all very well, but first you must avoid getting checkmated. The king is a sitting duck if the centre opens up before he has castled.

Seirawan-Zarnicki
Buenos Aires 1993

White has sacrificed a pawn for a lead in development, but his initiative will disappear unless he can stop his opponent castling into safety.

1 ♖xd6! ♕xd6 2 ♖d1 ♕c7

2...♕e7 3 ♘e5 ♗b7 (3...0-0 4 ♘xc6 ♕b7 5 ♕f3 offers no relief) 4 ♘xc6 ♕c7 5 ♗f4 ♕c8 is met by 6 ♕a4! ♘d7 7 ♗d6! and Black has no defence to 8 ♘e7.

3 ♗f4 ♕b7 4 ♘e5 ♗d7

4...♘d5!? (trying to block the diagonal by returning material) 5 ♘xc6! ♕xc6 6 cxd5 ♕b7 (6...exd5 7 ♗xd5 wins the rook) 7 dxe6! wins, as 7...♕xg2 fails to 8 exf7+ ♔e7 9 ♗g5+ ♔f8 10 ♖d8#; 4...0-0 5 ♗xc6 ♕b8 6 ♘g6 e5 7 ♗xe5 actually traps the queen.

5 ♖xd7!

White turns up the heat with a second exchange sacrifice, which had to be foreseen at the start of the combination.

5...♘xd7 6 ♗xc6 ♕a6 7 ♘xd7

Black's rooks can only watch as the white pieces devour their king.

7...♕c8

After 7...♔e7, 8 ♕d3! is best, pursuing the attack rather than grabbing the material.

8 ♗a4!?

8 ♘b8+ winning a whole rook is possible, but Seirawan plays for mate.

8...♔e7 9 ♕d3 f6 10 ♕d6+ ♔f7

10...♔e8 11 ♘e5+ mates quickly.

11 ♘e5+! fxe5

11...♔g8 12 ♗d7 is similar.

12 ♗d7 ♕d8 13 ♕xe6+ ♔f8 14 ♗xe5 g6 15 ♗f6 1-0

If the centre is firmly closed, however, the king may be safest where he is. The following example sees Seirawan on the receiving end of an audacious attack.

Seirawan-Beliavsky
Brussels 1988

12 ♘a4?

Aiming at the potential outpost on c5, but missing Black's brilliant reply. 12 ♘e5 is better, with equal chances.

12...g5!!

An unpleasant surprise: seeing that the centre is closed, Black leaves his king in the centre and launches a kingside pawn storm.

13 ♗g3 h5

Threatening ...h4 and ...f6, trapping the bishop. There is a similar thrust in the section on unpinning in Chapter 2.

14 h3 g4 15 hxg4 hxg4 16 ♘e5

16 ♘h2 ♘f6! 17 ♘c5 ♗xc5 18 dxc5 ♘e4 favours Black, as 19 ♘xg4? ♕g5 leads to a decisive attack.

16...♘xe5 17 ♗xe5 f6 18 ♗g3 ♔f7

Connecting the major pieces along the back rank and threatening to give mate on the h-file with ...♕g8-h7-h1.

19 ♖e1?!

19 f4 to give the king some air, or a humble retreat with 19 ♘c3, might be more tenacious.

19...♖h5 20 ♕d2?!

Hoping to sneak the king out of trouble via f1-e2-d1, but Black has other ideas.

20...♗e4! 21 ♔f1

21 ♘c3 ♕h8 22 ♔f1 ♖h1+ 23 ♔e2 ♖xe1+ 24 ♖xe1 ♗xg2 would prolong the game, but hardly improve White's chances.

21...♗f3! 0-1

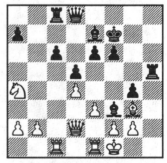

The king is trapped and mate is inevitable, e.g. 22 gxf3 gxf3 23 ♔g1 ♕h8, and ...♖h1# cannot be stopped.

If the kings castle on opposite sides of the board, the game becomes extremely sharp as each player launches a pawn storm on the opposing monarch. Time is of the essence, as the players desperately try to persuade each other to accept a pawn sacrifice!

Nezhmetdinov-Taimanov
USSR Ch ½f 1951

1 e4 c5 2 ♘f3 ♘c6 3 d4 cxd4 4 ♘xd4 ♘f6 5 ♘c3 d6 6 ♗g5 e6 7 ♕d2 ♗e7 8 0-0-0 0-0

9 ♘b3

9 ♗xf6 ♗xf6 10 ♘xc6 bxc6 11 ♕xd6 is a mistake, as it allows Black to seize the initiative with 11...♕b6!, when 12 ♕g3 ♖b8 13 b3 ♗xc3 14 ♕xc3 ♕xf2 regains the pawn with advantage – 15 ♕xc6 ♗b7 improves only Black's position.

9...♕b6 10 f3

10 ♗xf6 ♗xf6 11 ♕xd6 ♕xf2 is nothing special for White.

10...a6 11 ♗e3

Modern theory suggests that 11 h4! intending simply h5-h6 gives White an edge, as he forces a weakness before his opponent's counter-attack becomes dangerous.

11...♕c7 12 g4 b5 13 g5 ♘d7 14 f4 ♘b6 15 ♕f2 ♖b8 16 h4 ♘a4!?

16...b4 is more conventional, but Black was reluctant to allow the simplification 17 ♗xb6 ♕xb6 18 ♕xb6 ♖xb6 19 ♘a4 ♖b8 20 ♗g2.

17 ♗d2

17 ♘xa4 bxa4 would only help Black by opening the b-file.

17...♘xc3 18 ♗xc3 b4 19 ♗d2 a5 20 ♔b1

This move is often useful in similar situations: the king leaves the half-open c-file, and vacates c1 for the knight.

20...a4 21 ♘c1 ♗d7 22 ♗d3 ♖fc8 23 h5 ♘a5 24 f5 ♘c4 25 f6 ♗f8 26 g6!

A typical blow: White tries to force open as many lines as possible on the kingside.

26...♕c5!

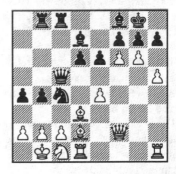

Offering the exchange of queens now that White has committed himself to the pawn storm.

27 gxh7+?!

27 ♕xc5 ♘xd2+ 28 ♖xd2 ♖xc5 29 gxf7+ ♔xf7 30 fxg7 ♗xg7 31 e5! ♗xe5 32 ♗xh7 is the most logical continuation, when the h-pawn should give White sufficient counterplay to hold the draw.

27...♔h8!

This is crucial to Black's defensive plan: the white pawn on h7 must be left alone, as it shields his king from attack.

28 ♕xc5

28 fxg7+ ♗xg7 29 ♕xc5 (29 ♕xf7? ♕d4!) 29...♖xc5 30 ♗xc4

♖xc4 31 ♗f4 is White's best chance, but in contrast to the previous note, Black will have connected passed pawns after the inevitable fall of the e4-pawn, after e.g. 31...♗c6 32 ♗xd6 ♖c8 33 h6 ♗f8 34 ♗xf8 ♖xf8.

28...♖xc5 29 ♗f4?!

29 ♗xc4 ♖xc4 30 fxg7+ ♗xg7 31 ♗f4 is the last chance to reach the previous note.

29...gxf6 30 ♘e2

30 ♗xc4 ♖xc4 31 ♗xd6 ♗xd6 32 ♖xd6 ♗c6 is very good for Black, for example 33 b3 axb3 34 axb3 ♗xe4 35 bxc4 ♗xh1 36 ♖d7 ♖b7 37 ♖xb7 ♗xb7 38 ♘d3 ♔xh7 and White's knight will be no match for the central pawn mass.

30...♘e5 31 ♗e3 ♖cc8 32 ♖hg1 ♔xh7 33 h6 b3!

Having taken time out to exchange queens and break up White's attack, Taimanov returns to the unfinished business on the queenside.

34 cxb3 axb3 35 a3 ♘xd3 36 ♖xd3 ♗b5 37 ♖d2 ♖c2! 38 ♘f4 ♖xd2 39 ♗xd2 ♗xh6

The ashes of White's burnt-out attack are easy pickings for the rampant bishops.

40 ♖h1 ♔g7 41 ♘xe6+ fxe6 42 ♗xh6+ ♔g6 43 ♗f4 e5 44 ♖g1+ ♔f7 45 ♗d2 ♗d3+ 0-1

After 46...♗xe4, Black's three connected passed pawns will be unstoppable.

Fischer-Spassky
Belgrade (25) 1992
1 e4 c5 2 ♘c3 ♘c6 3 ♘ge2 d6 4 d4 cxd4 5 ♘xd4 e6 6 ♗e3 ♘f6 7 ♕d2 ♗e7 8 f3 a6 9 0-0-0 0-0

Five consecutive zeros on the scoresheet means a fight.

10 g4

To kick away the chief defender, the knight on f6.

10...♘xd4 11 ♗xd4 b5 12 g5 ♘d7 13 h4 b4 14 ♘a4

It's always difficult to find the right balance between defence and attack. White had to decide between this, which leaves the knight vulnerable but halts the black a-pawn, and 14 ♘e2 and possibly ♘g3 joining the attack.

14...♗b7

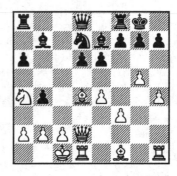

With a big threat of 15...♗c6 when 16 b3 would be forced and after 16...♗xa4 17 bxa4 White's defences are wrecked. However, 14...♕a5 15 b3 ♘c5 was better, since this meets with a surprising response:

15 ♘b6!!

15 ♕xb4 ♗c6 threatens ...♖b8 or ...e5 followed by ...d5 hitting the queen. In such situations it is rarely worth grabbing the pawn and conceding the initiative even if you cannot see a clear-cut win for the opponent. You should consider the

open lines to your king and the time involved taking the material.

15...♖b8

After 15...♘xb6 16 ♕xb4 ♖b8 17 ♗xb6 White would be a safe pawn up because his pieces suddenly control lots of queenside squares.

16 ♘xd7

White has exchanged off his one big problem, the knight, and he is ahead in the pawn race. Fischer plays the rest of the game faultlessly.

16...♕xd7 17 ♔b1!

Nearly always a good idea when you have played 0-0-0. The king is one square further from the centre and covers a2. In Sicilian positions the king also benefits from being off the c-file.

17...♕c7 18 ♗d3 ♗c8 19 h5 e5 20 ♗e3 ♗e6 21 ♖dg1

The rooks are ready for the inevitable opening of a kingside file after g6.

21...a5 22 g6

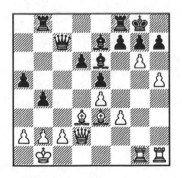

22...♗f6 23 gxh7+ ♔h8 24 ♗g5

Simply exchanging a defender.

24...♕e7 25 ♖g3 ♗xg5 26 ♖xg5 ♕f6 27 ♖hg1 ♕xf3

27...♔xh7 28 ♕g2 ♖g8 29 ♖g6 fxg6 30 hxg6+ ♔h8 31 ♕h2+.

28 ♖xg7

Threatening 29 ♖g8+ ♖xg8 30 hxg8♕+ ♖xg8 31 ♕h6 mate.

28...♕f6 29 h6 a4 30 b3

♕g2 will win anyway but playing it right away was more fun: 30 ♕g2 ♕d8 31 ♖g3 f6 (31...♕f6 32 ♖g8+ ♔xh7 33 ♖g7+ ♔h8 34 h7) 32 ♖h3 ♖b7 (32...♗xh3 33 ♕g7#) 33 ♕g7+!! ♖xg7 34 hxg7#.

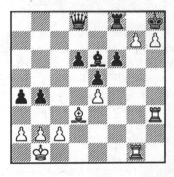

A variation pointed out by BCF International Director Simon Brown.

30...axb3 31 axb3 ♖fd8 32 ♕g2 ♖f8 33 ♖g8+ ♔xh7 34 ♖g7+ ♔h8 35 h7 1-0

With ♖g8+ White will finally bludgeon open both the h- and g-file and force mate.

The Bishop Pair

In an open position, the two bishops are a lethal weapon, especially if the opposing king is exposed. Material sacrifices may be necessary to release their full power, but cheap at the price:

Suetin-Wilson
Berlin 1991

Black has pushed forward on the kingside, hoping to build an attack around the strong bishop on f3. However, White's bishop pair points menacingly at the enemy king, and with his next move he generates a powerful initiative.

29 ♖bd1!! ♗xd1

The sacrifice must be accepted, but now Black's weaknesses are fatally exposed.

30 ♖xd1 ♕c8 31 ♕b5 ♘g6

31...♘g4 32 ♕d5 ♘e5 33 ♕xe4 is also good for White, e.g. 33...♘c6 34 ♕f3 ♘e5 (34...♘e6 35 ♗c3! seizes the long diagonal with the brutal threat of ♕f6-g7#) 35 ♕h5 ♖a6 36 ♘g4!! destroying Black's kingside – 36...♕xg4 loses to 37 ♗xf7+ ♔g7 38 ♕xg4 ♘xg4 39 ♗xe8.

32 ♗c3 ♘g4 33 ♖d7! ♘4e5

33...♖e7 34 ♘xg4 ♖xd7 35 ♕xd7 ♕xd7 36 ♘f6+ is hopeless. *(See diagram below)*.

34 ♗xf7+!

Black's position has been creaking for some time, and this new sacrifice brings it crashing down.

34...♘xf7 35 ♕f5!

Threatening both knights, not to mention 36 ♕f6.

35...♘ge5 36 ♗xe5 ♕xd7 37 ♕g6+!

37 ♕xd7 ♘xe5 allows Black to struggle on.

37...♔f8 38 ♗g7+1-0

It is mate in two: 38...♔g8 (38...♔e7 39 ♕f6#) 39 ♗xh6+ ♔h8 40 ♕g7#.

Opposite-Coloured Bishops

While opposite-coloured bishops may be the harbinger of a draw in the endgame, the exact opposite is true in the middlegame! In this case, the player with the initiative has a distinct advantage, as he can attack on squares of one colour with what amounts to an extra piece.

Babula-Blatny
Brno 1994

38 ♘e4!!

White sacrifices a whole piece to get his bishop into the attack. The threat of 39 ♘g5 means that the knight must be taken.

38...fxe4 39 ♗e6

Now White threatens 40 ♕xf7+ ♕xf7 41 ♖xe7, and, given half a chance (e.g. 39...♔f8), 40 ♖b8!. Black cannot defend his light squares.

39...♗f8 40 g4!

This is the clearest – now Black has the additional threat of g5-g6 to contend with.

40...♔g7 41 ♖b8! 1-0

Deflecting the queen; mate is forced after 41...♕xb8 42 ♕xf7+ ♔h8 43 ♕h5+ ♔g7 44 g5!.

Bad Bishop

Pein-Stepak
Ramat Hasharon 1990

1 d4 d6 2 ♘f3 ♗g4 3 c4 ♘d7 4 ♘c3 ♘gf6 5 e4 e5 6 ♗e2 ♗e7 7 ♗e3 0-0 8 d5 b6

In this position I exchanged off Black's good bishop with:

9 ♘d2 ♗xe2 10 ♕xe2 ♘xe4

Black should have tried to swap his bad bishop with 10...♘e8 and 11...♗g5.

11 ♘dxe4 f5 12 0-0

12 ♘d2 f4 wins the bishop.

12...fxe4 13 ♘xe4 ♘c5?

A bad mistake; after...

14 ♗xc5 bxc5

...I played my knight to e4 and it was far superior to the black bishop. By exchanging rooks and queens I reached the position on page 44 and won easily.

Use Your Rooks!

The above advice might sound trivial, but many players seem to become so absorbed in their plans that they forget about the rook, leaving him to doze peacefully in the corner. It's true that the rook is a heavy sleeper, but that's no reason not to wake him!

The rook needs open and half-open files; if none arise to begin with, it is essential to take active steps to create some.

The next game is a marvellous example of how to use your rooks from my good friend Peter Wells, who has had many fine games published in the *DT* chess column.

Wells-R.Grünberg
London 1984

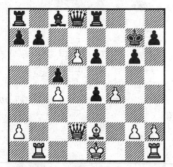

White has sacrificed a pawn, but has ample compensation with his lead in development and strong d6-pawn. In addition, the exchange of dark-squared bishops has weakened Black's king position.

19 h4! b6

19...e3 (19...h5 20 g4 hxg4 21 h5 opens even more lines) 20 ♕c3+ ♕f6 21 ♕e5 b6 22 h5 ♖f8 23 hxg6 hxg6 24 ♖b3 favoured White in Kouatly-Cocozza, Thessaloniki OL 1984.

20 h5 ♖f8 21 hxg6 hxg6 22 ♖b3!

Preparing to swing over to the h-file.

22...♕f6 23 ♖bh3 ♕d4 24 ♖h7+ ♔f6

24...♔g8? gets mated after 25 ♕xd4 cxd4 26 ♖h8+ ♔f7 27 ♖1h7+ ♔e8 (27...♔f6 28 ♖xf8#) 28 ♖e7+ ♔d8 29 ♖xf8#.

25 g4!

Even an exchange of queens will not save the black king.

25...♕xd2+ 26 ♔xd2 e5

Creating some breathing space for the king.

27 ♖f1 ♖d8

27...♔e6 28 fxe5 ♖e8 (28...♖xf1 29 ♖e7#) 29 ♖f8! ♗d7 30 ♖ff7! wins a piece or mates.

28 g5+ ♔e6

28...♔f5 29 ♖f7+ ♔e6 30 ♖f6+ ♔d7 31 fxe5 is crushing.

29 ♔e3 exf4+

29...♖xd6 30 ♗g4#, while 29...♔xd6 30 ♖d1+ picks up the rook.

30 ♔xe4?

This allows Black a surprising resource, overlooked by both players. Instead, 30 ♖xf4! ♔e5 31 ♖f6 ♖d7 (31...♖xd6 32 ♖e7+ ♔e6 33 ♗g4 wins a piece) 32 ♖e7+ ♖xe7 33 dxe7 ♗d7 34 ♗g4! ♗xg4 (34...♗a4 35 ♖e6#) 35 ♖f8 is a winning ending for White.

30...♔xd6?

30...♖h8!! equalises, for example 31 ♖xh8 (31 ♖g7 ♖g8!) 31...♗b7+ 32 ♔xf4 ♖xh8 33 ♖d1 ♖f8+ 34 ♔e3 ♖d8 35 ♗g4+ ♔e5 36 d7 ♗c6 and White cannot improve his position.

31 ♖d1+ ♔c6 32 ♖xd8 ♗f5+ 33 ♔e5! 1-0

33...♖xd8 34 ♗f3+ mates in two more moves.

Kotov-Steiner
USSR-USA 1955

White has more space and the better minor piece and he uses these advantages to launch a pawn storm backed up by his rooks.

25 ♖f3!

The obvious plan of opening the f-file with 25 f5 would rebound, as the half-open e-file will be just as useful to Black. Instead, Kotov plans a methodical build-up in the g-file.

25...♘d6 26 g4 ♖f8 27 ♔h1 ♔h8 28 ♖g1 ♕d8 29 ♖fg3 ♖d7

Black's only possibility of counterplay, ...♘e4, is impossible as White has total control of the b1-h7 diagonal.

30 g5 ♘f5

30...hxg5 31 ♖xg5 changes nothing.

31 ♗xf5 exf5

31...♖xf5 32 gxh6 gxh6 33 ♕g2 ♖f8 34 ♖g6 ♖h7 35 ♖g7 is crushing.

32 gxh6 gxh6 33 ♕g2 ♖df7?

33...♕e8 is relatively best, although White should win the ending after 34 ♖g6 ♕e4 35 ♖xh6+ ♖h7 36 ♖xh7+ ♔xh7 37 ♕xe4 fxe4 (37...dxe4 38 ♖g5 is totally submissive) 38 ♖g5.

34 ♖g6!

34 ♖g7 ♕e8 35 ♕g6? (35 ♔h2! still wins) 35...♕e4+ 36 ♔h2 ♕c2+ 37 ♖g2 ♕xg2+! 38 ♕xg2 ♖xg7 gives away all White's advantage.

34...♕e7

34...♖h7 35 ♖g7 and 34...♖f6 35 ♖xh6+! are no better.

35 ♖g8+ 1-0

The attack down the g-file is crowned with mate next move.

Pawn Structure

The pawn structure that arises out of the opening more often than not defines the middlegame plans for both sides. There are four kinds of pawn constellation or islands that we will consider.

Doubled Pawns

Doubled pawns have both positive and negative features. On the plus side, a line is opened for the rooks, and the pawns may control more important squares when doubled. On the other hand, doubled pawns may be weak, especially if they are isolated or on a half-open file – or both. Doubled pawns may cripple a pawn majority when it comes to generating a passed pawn in the endgame.

Botvinnik-Kan
USSR Ch (Leningrad) 1939
1 d4 ♘f6 2 c4 e6 3 ♘c3 ♗b4 4 ♘f3 c5 5 a3 ♗xc3+ 6 bxc3 ♕a5

This is over-ambitious; after 6...b6, intending ...♗a6, ...♘c6-a5, the c4-pawn is in danger – see the next game.

7 ♗d2 ♘e4 8 ♕c2 ♘xd2 9 ♘xd2 d6 10 e3 e5

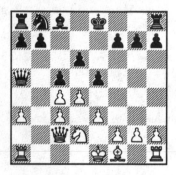

11 dxe5!

A surprising move, voluntarily isolating his doubled pawns, but Botvinnik has seen that he can plant his bishop on the d5-square.

11...dxe5 12 ♗d3 h6 13 0-0 0-0 14 f4 ♘d7

The open e-file after 14...exf4 15 exf4 only accelerates White's kingside attack.

15 f5 ♘f6 16 ♘e4 ♕d8 17 ♘xf6+ ♕xf6 18 ♗e4 ♖b8 19 ♖ad1 b6 20 h3 ♗a6 21 ♗d5

Botvinnik's opening strategy has been an unqualified success: the bishop dominates the position from its secure outpost on d5.

21...b5

Black is so passive that he even liquidates the doubled pawns in search of some play for his pieces.

22 cxb5 ♖xb5 23 c4 ♖b6 24 ♖b1 ♖d8 25 ♖xb6 axb6

The backward pawn becomes a serious liability on the half-open b-file.

26 e4 ♗c8 27 ♕a4 ♗d7 28 ♕a7 ♗e8 29 ♖b1 ♖d6 30 a4

Botvinnik decides to exploit the awkward placing of Black's major pieces by transferring his attack to the c5-pawn.

30...♔h7

Black has no better way to prepare for 31 a5, as 30...♕d8 31 a5 bxa5 32 ♖b8 ♕d7 33 ♕xd7 ♖xd7 34 ♖xe8+ loses a piece.

31 a5 bxa5 32 ♕xa5 ♖a6 33 ♕xc5

and White won.

A.Williams-Dzindzichashvili
Thessaloniki OL 1984

1 d4 ♘f6 2 c4 e6 3 ♘c3 ♗b4 4 a3

This committal move is not very popular nowadays. One popular alternative developed by Rubinstein is to play e3 and ♘e2 to prevent the doubling of the pawns.

4...♗xc3+ 5 bxc3 b6

Black sets about winning the c4-pawn and makes it look so easy. I have to confess I laughed out loud the first time I saw the game. A few years later I also got outplayed by the Djin. Ironically he allowed me to give him doubled pawns, which later took on a diamond shape on e3, d4, e5 and f4; his bishop sat in the middle on e4 and dominated the board.

6 f3 ♗a6 7 e4

White dominates the centre but Black is unconcerned.

7...♘c6 8 ♗g5 ♕c8!

This move conceals the true intention. Black can allow ♗xf6 doubling his pawn because his king would be quite safe on the queenside and he might attack down the open g-file.

9 ♗d3 ♘a5 10 ♕e2 ♕b7

It's that simple. Black goes to c6 and removes the c4-pawn in broad daylight.

11 ♘h3 ♕c6 12 0-0 ♗xc4 13 ♘f2 ♗xd3 14 ♕xd3 ♕c4 15 ♕e3 ♘g8!

Finally deciding to castle kingside and after **16 ♖ad1 f6 17 ♗h4 ♘e7 18 ♗g3 0-0** Black was a healthy pawn up and won in 45 moves.

This game illustrates how doubled and isolated pawns can be so vulnerable in the endgame.

Pinter-Timman

Las Palmas IZ 1982

1 d4 ♘f6 2 c4 e6 3 ♘c3 ♗b4 4 ♘f3 c5 5 e3 ♘c6 6 ♗d3 ♗xc3+

Note that in this variation Black does not even wait to be asked by the move a3 before capturing the knight.

7 bxc3 d6 8 0-0 e5

Black's strategy here is to set up a firm blockade on the dark squares before doing anything else.

9 ♘d2 0-0

The pawn sacrifice should be ignored: 9...cxd4 10 cxd4 exd4 11 exd4 ♘xd4 12 ♖e1+ ♘e6 13 ♗a3 gave White excellent compensation in Portisch-Timman, Wijk aan Zee 1978.

10 d5 ♘e7 11 f3 ♗f5!?

An interesting idea, provoking e4 to clarify the central pawn position. White's plan of f4 only works if he can recapture on f4 with a pawn, as otherwise the e5-square will be an excellent outpost for a black knight.

12 e4 ♗d7 13 ♕c2 ♘h5!

Menacing the weakened kingside dark squares; a future ...♘g6 is a distinct possibility.

14 g3 f5 15 exf5 ♗xf5 16 ♘e4 h6

Preventing the annoying ♘g5-e6; now 17 g4 ♗xe4 and 18...♘f4 is awful for White, who has no way of activating his bishops.

17 ♗d2 ♕d7 18 ♖ae1 ♗h3 19 ♖f2 ♖f7 20 ♕d1 ♘f6 21 ♗e3 ♘xe4 22 ♗xe4 ♗f5!

Black's plan is simply to exchange into an endgame where his knight will mop up the doubled pawns.

23 ♕c2 ♖af8 24 ♖ef1 ♗xe4 25 ♕xe4 ♕f5 26 a4?!

White's position is bad enough, without serving his queenside pawns up on a platter.

26...♕xe4 27 fxe4 ♖xf2 28 ♖xf2 ♖xf2 29 ♔xf2 a5!

The knight is only two short hops from b6, and the a4-pawn is a goner.

30 ♔e2 ♘c8 31 ♔d3 ♘b6 32 h4 ♘xa4 33 ♗c1 ♘b6 34 g4 ♔f7 35 ♗d2 a4 36 ♗c1

White's last hope is to prevent the black king penetrating his position, but it is not to be.

36...♔f6 37 ♗a3 g5

Fixing White's kingside pawns on light squares, so that a subsequent ...♘d7-f6 will tie his king to f3.

38 h5 ♔e7 39 ♗c1 ♘d7 40 ♔e2 ♘f6 41 ♔f3 ♔d7 0-1

A possible continuation is 42 ♗a3 ♔c7 43 ♗c1 ♔b6 44 ♗b2 ♔a5 45 ♗a3 b6 46 ♗c1 a3! 47 ♗xa3 ♔a4 48 ♗c1 ♔b3 and ...♔xc4 intending ...♔d3 finishes off White's resistance.

The Isolated Queen's Pawn

The assessment of positions with an isolated queen's pawn depends very much on who has the initiative. An IQP confers an advantage in space, as well as influence over two squares in the enemy camp, c5 and more importantly e5 from where a knight may well spearhead a kingside attack. The player with the IQP is usually obliged to attack. However, if the pawn can be securely blockaded, the attack beaten off and pieces (especially the queens) exchanged, it becomes a serious liability in the endgame – not to mention the square in front of it. The strategic battle often revolves around the struggle for the square in front of the pawn, if a knight lands there it cannot be shifted and the IQP will be blockaded. If the owner of the IQP can advance it such an advance usually wreaks havoc.

Kamsky-Short
Linares Ct (5) 1994

1 d4 ♘f6 2 c4 e6 3 ♘c3 ♗b4 4 e3 c5 5 ♗d3 ♘c6 6 ♘e2

The Rubinstein plan.

6...cxd4 7 exd4 d5 8 cxd5

After 8 a3, Black gains a tempo with 8...dxc4 9 ♗xc4 ♗e7. White's bishop belongs on the b1-h7 diagonal.

8...♘xd5

Better than 8...exd5, when White finds it easier to pressurise his opponent's d-pawn: the knight on e2 can move to f4, and the attempted pin with ...♗g4 can be met by f3.

9 0-0 ♗d6 10 ♘e4

10 a3 ♕h4! allows Black serious counterplay.

10...♗e7 11 a3

This is an important precaution against ...♘b4, as White intends ♗c2 and ♕d3 to provoke a weakness on the kingside.

11...0-0 12 ♗c2 ♖e8

12...e5!? reveals the dark side of the knight's position on e2: the d4-pawn is liquidated, and with it go White's space advantage and attacking chances. The continuation 13 dxe5 ♘xe5 14 ♘f4 ♘xf4 15 ♗xf4 ♘g6 16 ♗e3 ♗e6 was completely equal in Malishauskas-Serper, Beskidy 1991.

13 ♕d3 g6

Black will probably have to play this some time, due to the veiled threat against h7, so he does it at once and avoids unnecessary weakenings such as ...h6 or ...f5.

14 ♗h6 b6 15 ♖ad1 ♗b7 16 ♖fe1 ♖c8

Black has completed his development, and has the d4-pawn under heavy restraint. However, he has not yet exchanged any pieces, and he remains slightly cramped and passive.

17 ♗b3

The bishop has done its work on the b1-h7 diagonal, and is now needed in the fight for d5.

17...a6

17...♘a5 18 ♗a2 ♘f6 19 ♘xf6+ ♗xf6 20 ♘f4 intending b4, driving back the knight and taking control of d5, favours White; the defensive try 20...♗g5 fails to 21 ♘xe6! fxe6 (21...♖xe6 22 ♖xe6 ♗xh6 23 ♖xg6+!) 22 ♖xe6 ♖xe6 23 ♗xe6+ ♔h8 24 ♗xc8 as Black's scattered pieces will struggle against the powerful white d-pawn.

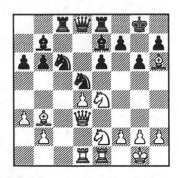

18 ♘2g3 ♘b8?!

18...♘a5 19 ♗a2 f5 20 ♘c3 ♗f6 is better, with balanced chances. Although e6 is very weak Black can play ...b5 and ...♘c4 to blot out the bishop on a2.

19 ♕f3 ♖c7?

Intending ...♖d7 to attack the IQP but under-estimating Kamsky's attacking chances; better is 19...♗h4, meeting 20 ♘h5 with 20...gxh5, as 21 ♕g3+ is now impossible.

20 ♘h5!

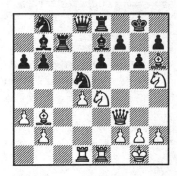

20...♘d7

20...f5 21 ♘c3 favours White, e.g. 21...♕d7 (21...♘xc3? 22 ♗xe6+ ♔h8 23 ♗g7#) 22 ♖xe6!! ♖xc3 (22...♕xe6 23 ♘xd5 leaves Black defenceless) 23 bxc3 ♕xe6 24 ♘g7 ♕d7 25 ♘xe8 with a decisive material advantage.

21 h4! ♘7f6

21...♗xh4 22 ♘d6 ♖e7 23 ♖e4! and now Black gets mated after 23...gxh5 24 ♖g4+! ♔h8 (24...hxg4 25 ♕xg4+ mates in two) 25 ♕xf7!.

21...♕a8 22 ♗xd5 ♗xd5 23 ♘hf6+ ♘xf6 24 ♘xf6+ ♔h8 (24...♗xf6 25 ♕xf6 and 26 ♕g7#) 25 ♘xd5 ♕xd5 26 ♕xf7 wins.

22 ♘hxf6+ ♘xf6 23 d5!

A thematic breakthrough: the sacrifice of the isolated pawn unleashes the full power of the pieces massed behind it.

23...♘xe4

23...♘xd5 24 ♗xd5 ♗xd5 25 ♖xd5! exd5 26 ♘f6+ ♔h8 (26...♗xf6 27 ♖xe8+ ♕xe8 28 ♕xf6 with the familiar mate on g7) 27 ♘xe8 ♕xe8 28 ♕f6+! ♗xf6 29 ♖xe8#.

24 dxe6 f5

Short has nothing better than to give up his queen, as 25 exf7+ is an even bigger threat.

25 ♖xd8 ♖xd8 26 ♖d1 1-0

Material down, Black is also faced with threats such as ♖d7 and ♕f4-e5.

Now the down side: the pawn is blockaded and very weak in an endgame.

G.Kuzmin-Uhlmann
Leningrad 1973

1 e4 e6 2 d4 d5 3 ♘d2 c5 4 ♘gf3 ♘c6 5 exd5 exd5 6 ♗b5 ♗d6 7 dxc5 ♗xc5 8 0-0 ♘ge7 9 ♘b3 ♗d6 10 ♗g5 0-0 11 ♗h4!?

The king's bishop is usually the IQP holder's strongest minor piece – compare Kamsky-Short – so White prepares ♗g3 to contest the dark squares.

11...♗g4

Kuzmin had lost with 11...♕c7 in an earlier round against Karpov.

12 ♗e2 ♕b6 13 ♗xe7!? ♘xe7

13...♗xe7!? 14 ♕xd5 a5 with good counterplay for the pawn is more combative.

14 ♕d4!

Forcing the exchange of queens, after which Black's bishop pair does not fully compensate for his isolated d-pawn – the knight entrenched on d4 sees to that.

14...♕xd4 15 ♘fxd4 ♗d7 16 ♖ad1 ♖fd8 17 ♖fe1 ♔f8 18 c3 a5 19 a3 a4 20 ♘a1!

The knight is re-routed to attack d5 directly.

20...♘c8 21 ♘ac2 ♘b6 22 ♘e3 ♗f4 23 ♘dc2 ♗e6 24 ♖d4

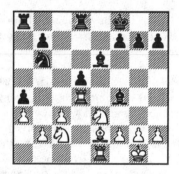

24...♗xe3?

There is no need to make this concession, as after 24...♗d6 25 ♖ed1 ♗c5 26 ♖4d2 ♔e7 27 ♗f3, the d-pawn can be saved by 27...♖d7! thanks to the potential pin on the d-file: 28 ♘xd5+?? (28 ♗xd5? ♖ad8 29 c4 ♘xc4! 30 ♘xc4 ♖xd5 favours Black) 28...♗xd5 29 ♗xd5 loses a piece after 29...♖ad8. Although Black is completely passive if the d5-pawn is declined, he still has his bishops and the onus is on White to find a way to make progress. In fact two years later, in what turned out to be a WCC final because of Fischer's abdication, Korchnoi held Karpov at bay on the black side of these positions by keeping his dark-squared bishop active throughout and it was always more than a match for a Karpov knight. Logically, the bishop that covers the square in front of the IQP is the one you want to keep. I quote from the tournament book by Wade, Blackstock, & Kotov, one of the best tournament books ever written – try to get a second-hand copy if you can. I studied it so intently as a youngster it was confiscated by my maths teacher no less than three times during class. The authors write "Parting with the two bishops in such a position is to be considered only in emergencies or where a tangible advantage can be secured. In this instance neither applies."

25 ♘xe3 ♘c4 26 ♖ed1! ♖dc8

Abandoning the d-pawn in the hope of obtaining some counterplay. 26...♔e7 (26...♘xb2? 27 ♖1d2 wins the knight, which can be taken for free if it retreats to c4) 27 ♗xc4 dxc4 28 ♖xd8 ♖xd8 29 ♖xd8 ♔xd8 30 f4 gives Black a dreadful ending, with his pawns fixed on the same colour squares as his bishop.

27 ♘xd5 ♘xb2 28 ♖b1 ♗xd5 29 ♖xd5 ♘c4 30 ♖xb7 ♘a5

30...♘xa3 31 ♖dd7 and Black has no answer to the doubled rooks rampaging along the seventh rank.

31 ♖bb5 ♘c4 32 ♖d7 g6 33 f4 ♖a6 34 ♖b4 ♖ac6 35 ♗d3 ♔g7 36 ♖d4 ♘xa3 37 c4

Now the knight is trapped.

37...♖a6 38 ♔f2 ♖a5 39 ♔e3 ♖c7 40 ♔d2 h5 41 ♖e4 ♖d7 42 ♖e1 ♖c5 43 ♖c1 ♖d4 44 ♔e3 1-0

Even the ingenious 44...♖cd5 does not save the knight after 45 ♗e2 f5 46 ♔f3 and 47 ♖c3.

Hanging Pawns

Hanging pawns are normally strongest when they stand side by side, keeping their options open. As soon as one steps out of line, a gaping hole opens up in front of the other, and a blockade on this square can be extremely bad news. However, if they can be maintained in their preferred position, they secure a large advantage in space. The player facing hanging pawns should try to exchange some pieces – typically the queens and a couple of minor pieces – to relieve his cramp, park his rooks on the half-open files and manoeuvre against the pawns with his remaining minor pieces.

Korchnoi-Karpov
Merano Wch (1) 1981

1 c4 e6 2 ♘c3 d5 3 d4 ♗e7 4 ♘f3 ♘f6 5 ♗g5 h6 6 ♗h4 0-0 7 e3 b6 8 ♖c1 ♗b7 9 ♗e2 ♘bd7 10 cxd5 exd5 11 0-0 c5 12 dxc5

A more recent discovery is 12 ♕a4 (intending 13 ♗a6) 12...a6, provoking an extra weakness before entering the hanging pawns scenario with 13 dxc5 bxc5.

12...bxc5 13 ♕c2 ♖c8 14 ♖fd1 ♕b6 15 ♕b1?!

15 ♗g3 ♖fd8 16 b3 has been suggested as an improvement, but already it is White who has to play accurately for equality!

15...♖fd8 16 ♖c2 ♕e6

17 ♗g3

17 ♖cd2 ♘e4! 18 ♘xe4 dxe4 19 ♗xe7 exf3 20 ♗xd8 fxe2 21 ♖xe2 (21 ♖xd7 ♕g4 22 ♖1d5 ♗xd5 23 ♖xd5 ♕e4! leaves Black the exchange ahead) 21...♗e4 22 ♕c1 ♖xd8 clearly favours Black.

17...♘h5 18 ♖cd2 ♘xg3 19 hxg3 ♘f6 20 ♕c2 g6 21 ♕a4 a6 22 ♗d3 ♔g7 23 ♗b1

White is desperately trying to find squares for his pieces, but it is a real struggle with the hanging pawns dominating the centre.

23...♕b6 24 a3 d4!

Just as in Kamsky-Short, this typical sacrifice leads to a ferocious attack.

25 ♘e2

25 exd4 ♗c6! 26 ♕c2 (26 dxc5 ♗xa4 27 cxb6 ♗xd1 picks up an exchange) 26...♗xf3 27 gxf3 (27 dxc5 ♗xd1) 27...cxd4 28 ♘a4 ♕b5 wins the knight.

25...dxe3 26 fxe3 c4! 27 ♘ed4 ♕c7 28 ♘h4

28 ♘e2 ♗c5 29 ♘fd4 ♕e5 leaves Black in total control.

28...♕e5

28...♕xg3?? loses the queen after 29 ♘hf5+ gxf5 30 ♘xf5+.

29 ♔h1 ♔g8 30 ♘df3 ♕xg3

Winning a pawn, with a continuing attack against White's exposed king.

31 ♖xd8+ ♗xd8 32 ♕b4 ♗e4 33 ♗xe4 ♘xe4 34 ♖d4 ♘f2+ 35 ♔g1 ♘d3 36 ♕b7 ♖b8 37 ♕d7 ♗c7 38 ♔h1

38 ♖xc4 ♕f2+ 39 ♔h1 ♕f1+ 40 ♘g1 ♘f2#.

38...♖xb2 39 ♖xd3 cxd3 40 ♕xd3 ♕d6

40...g5! attacks the knight that defends g2, and thereby wins a piece. Karpov's choice, probably made in time pressure, is less incisive but still wins easily.

41 ♕e4 ♕d1+ 42 ♘g1 ♕d6 43 ♘hf3 ♖b5 0-1

Weak squares and backward pawns

Any square which cannot be defended by a pawn may become weak – as Tarrasch used to say, every pawn move creates a new weakness. Rubinstein-Salwe above is a particularly gruesome example of what happens to people who give up their weak squares without a fight. The knight is the piece best suited to occupying a weak central square, as it 'attacks the parts other pieces cannot reach'!

Geller-Fedorowicz
New York Open 1990
1 e4 c5 2 ♘f3 ♘c6 3 d4 cxd4 4 ♘xd4 ♘f6 5 ♘c3 e5

The Sicilian Pelikan. Black claims his share of space in the centre, gaining time against the knight into the bargain, but leaves a gaping hole on d5.

6 ♘db5 d6 7 ♗g5

Pinning the main defender of d5.

7...a6 8 ♘a3 b5 9 ♗xf6 gxf6

This is necessary, as White gets too far ahead in development after 9...♕xf6 10 ♘d5.

10 ♘d5 ♗g7 11 c3 f5 12 exf5 ♗xf5 13 ♘c2 ♗e6 14 ♘ce3 ♘e7 15 g3

White develops all his minor pieces towards the key square.

15...♘xd5 16 ♘xd5 0-0 17 ♗g2 a5

17...♖b8 18 ♘b4 is awkward, threatening 19 ♘xa6 and 19 ♘c6.

18 0-0 ♖b8 19 ♕h5 ♔h8 20 ♖ad1 f5 21 ♖d2 ♕d7 22 ♖fd1

Doubling up against the backward d6-pawn.

22...♕f7 23 ♕h4

The exchange of queens would help Black to free his position since he has the weaker king.

23...e4

Desperate to release his dark-squared bishop, Black gives himself another hole on f4, which is promptly occupied.

24 ♘f4 ♗e5

24...♗xa2 25 ♖xd6 threatens 26 ♘g6+, winning the exchange, and 26 ♖d7, invading the seventh rank.

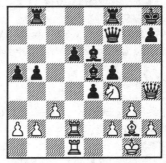

25 ♖xd6! ♗xd6 26 ♖xd6

The exchange sacrifice has eliminated the dark-squared bishop – now Black's good bishop! – and leaves the knight unassailable on its new outpost at f4.

26...♖fe8 27 g4!

Undermining the key e4-pawn. Geller's play follows the teachings of Nimzowitsch to the letter: the black centre is restrained, blockaded, and finally destroyed.

27...b4

27...fxg4 28 ♗xe4 is a winning attack for White, e.g. 28...♗xa2 29 ♗xh7! ♕xh7 30 ♖h6.

28 cxb4 Ξbc8

After 28...♗xa2 White can choose between 29 gxf5 Ξxb4 (29...♕xf5 30 ♘g6+ ♔g7 31 ♗h3 ♕f3 32 ♘f4) 30 Ξd8, 29 h3, 29 bxa5 fxg4 and 29 Ξf6 ♕d7 30 h3.

29 h3 fxg4

29...♗xa2.

30 ♕g5 gxh3

30...♗xa2.

31 ♕e5+ ♔g8 32 ♕g5+ ♔h8 33 ♕e5+ ♔g8 34 ♗xe4 ♗xa2 35 ♕g5+ ♕g7 36 ♗xh7+ ♔h8

36...♔xh7 37 Ξg6.

37 ♗g6 Ξe5 38 ♕h4+ ♔g8 39 ♔h2 ♕e7 40 ♗h7+ ♔f7 41 ♗g6+ ♔g8 42 Ξf6 ♔g7 43 ♗f5 1-0

43...Ξxf5 (43...♕xf6 44 ♘h5+ wins the queen) 44 ♕h6+ ♔g8 45 Ξxf5 with 46 Ξg7+ to follow removes most of Black's pieces.

Another game from the same defence. Don't get the idea that I am condemning the Pelikan – far from it. It often gives Black very dynamic chances. Indeed, a game between the same two players at the same tournament a year earlier went in favour of Black.

Short-Kramnik
Novgorod 1995

1 e4 c5 2 ♘f3 ♘c6 3 d4 cxd4 4 ♘xd4 ♘f6 5 ♘c3 e5 6 ♘db5 d6 7 ♗g5 a6 8 ♘a3 b5 9 ♗xf6 gxf6 10 ♘d5 ♗g7 11 c3

This is a useful move, clearing a path for the a3-knight to take part in the struggle for d5.

11...f5 12 exf5 ♗xf5 13 ♘c2 ♗e6 14 g3 0-0 15 ♗g2 Ξb8 16 0-0 ♕d7

16...♘e7 looks consistent, but in Short-Illescas, Madrid 1995, White gained the upper hand with 17 ♘xe7+ ♕xe7 18 ♘b4 Ξb6 19 f4! f5 20 ♗d5 (the exchange of bishops will strengthen White's grip on d5, as the last remaining black minor piece cannot possibly contest this square!) 20...a5 21 ♗xe6+ ♕xe6 22 ♘d5.

17 a4!

The knight on d5 will not win the game by itself, so White creates another weakness in his opponent's position.

17...b4

17...bxa4 is the natural move here, but 18 Ξxa4 a5 (18...Ξxb2 19 Ξxa6 ♗xd5 20 ♗xd5 ♘e7 21 ♘e3 leaves White clearly in command, although the liquidation of Black's queenside pawns gives him fair chances of holding the draw) 19 ♘ce3! Ξxb2 20 Ξc4! (intending 21 Ξxc6 and 22 ♘e7+) 20...Ξc8 21 ♕h5 is not altogether pleasant for Black, for example 21...f5 22 g4!? fxg4 23 ♗e4 h6 24 ♘f5 ♔f8 (24...♗xd5? 25 ♗xd5+ is absolutely suicidal) 25 ♕g6 (threatening 26 ♘xg7) 25...♕f7 26 ♕xf7+ ♗xf7 27 ♘xd6 wins material.

18 ②cxb4 ②xb4 19 cxb4 ♗xd5
20 ♗xd5 ♖xb4 21 b3 a5
21...♖d4 22 ♕f3 changes nothing,
while 21...e4 22 ♖a2 only gives
Black another weakness to worry
about.
22 ♕e2 e4
22...♗f6!? is an interesting attempt to activate the bishop, but
White can continue to improve his
position with simple moves: 23
♖ad1 ♗d8 24 ♗c4 ♕e7 25 f4! (the
centre has been immobilised, so it is
time to set about its destruction)
25...♗b6+ 26 ♔g2 ♔h8 27 fxe5
dxe5 28 ♖d5 and now 28...f6?! allows 29 ♖xe5! fxe5 30 ♖xf8+ ♕xf8
31 ♕xe5+ ♕g7 32 ♕e8+ mating.
23 ♖ad1 ♕e7 24 ♗c4 ♔h8
Escaping the pin in order to play
...f5.
25 ♖d5 f5
Now Short played 26 ♖fd1?!, winning only after some unnecessary
complications. Best, as he pointed
out afterwards, is 26 f4!, snuffing out
Black's counterplay: 26...♕c7 27
♖fd1 ♖f6 28 ♕h5 and Black can no
longer defend his weaknesses at f5,
a5 and d6.
26 ♖xa5 is also possible, when
26...f4?! 27 gxf4 ♖xf4 28 ♖a8+
gives White a strong initiative, e.g.
28...♖f8 29 ♖xf8+ ♗xf8 30 ♕g4
♗g7 31 ♖e1 and e4 drops off.

Backward Pawns

"A backward pawn can be defined
as a pawn that has been left behind
by the neighbouring pawns and can
no longer be supported by them" –

GM Ludek Pachman in *Complete
Chess Strategy 2*. All three volumes
in this series are classics in my view
but all are out of print – see your
second-hand dealer!

Fischer-Barczay
Sousse IZ 1967
1 e4 e5 2 ②f3 ②c6 3 ♗b5
The Ruy Lopez. Fischer used to
say 1 e4 was best by test, and he
almost invariably played the Lopez.
**3...a6 4 ♗a4 ②f6 5 0-0 ♗e7 6 ♖e1
b5 7 ♗b3 d6 8 c3 0-0 9 h3 ②b8**
The Breyer Defence, invented by
Gyula Breyer, one of the Hypermod-
ernists. Black creates a tough defensive set-up on the kingside after
...②bd7.
10 d4 ②bd7 11 ②h4
Aiming for f5.
11...exd4 12 cxd4 ②b6 13 ②f3
13 ②f5 ♗xf5 would ruin White's
pawns but he has a good pawn centre
and retreats the knight to support it.
**13...d5 14 e5 ②e4 15 ②bd2 ②xd2
16 ♗xd2 ♗f5 17 ♗c2 ♗xc2 18
♕xc2 ♖c8 19 b3**
Absolutely not 19 b4 which would
allow Black to cover his weaknesses
with ②c4.

19...♘d7

Black's c7-pawn is backward but cannot be freed with 19...c5 because of 20 dxc5 ♗xc5 21 ♕d3 threatening ♘g5 and after 21...h6, 22 ♗a5 is an extremely annoying pin, e.g. 22...♕d7 23 ♖ac1 ♗a3 24 ♖xc8 ♘xc8 25 b4 ♗b2 26 ♕b3 trapping the bishop.

20 e6! fxe6 21 ♖xe6 c5

21...♘b6 22 ♖ae1 ♗f6 23 ♗a5 (Pachman) with the idea of ♖c6 and ♖1c1 when the backward pawn is doomed.

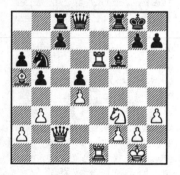

22 ♗a5 ♕xa5 23 ♖xe7 ♕d8 24 ♘g5 1-0

White threatens 25 ♕xh7 mate and 25 ♖xg7+ ♔xg7 26 ♘e6+ winning the queen, so Black resigned.

Pawn Islands

A cluster of pawns is known as a pawn 'island', and a player's pawn structure tends to be weaker the more islands it comprises.

Hug-Karpov
Bath TV 1977

The point of White's restrained formation in the diagram below is to strike back against the black centre with d4 or b4, but he is still a long way from achieving this.

This game was played in the BBC *Master Game* series, some of the best chess there has ever been on TV. The players explained their thoughts afterwards but it was done as if they were talking during the game and most people were taken in. If only they would repeat it. It must be such cheap TV and viewing figures for chess have always been respectable. A barrage of letters to Alan Yentob at the BBC please.

15 ♘e4 ♕e7 16 ♘fd2 f5

Karpov increases his spatial advantage.

17 ♘g3 f4 18 ♘gf1 fxe3 19 fxe3 ♘5f6 20 ♗f3 e4!

This advance forces White to compromise his pawn structure.

21 ♘xe4 ♘xe4 22 ♗xe4 ♗xe4 23 ♕c4+ ♕e6 24 dxe4

24 ♕xe4 ♕xb3 25 ♕c4+ (25 ♕f5? ♕xb2 26 ♕xd7 ♕xa3 wins a pawn) 25...♕xc4 26 ♖xc4 ♘e5 favours Black.

24...♕xc4 25 bxc4

25 ♖xc4 b5 regains the pawn with advantage.

25...Ïxe4

Now White has four pawn 'islands', in contrast to Black's two.

26 Ïed1 ♘f8 27 Ïd3 Ïce8 28 ♔f2 ♗e5

White's bishop is a useful defensive piece, so Black takes the opportunity to exchange it off.

29 ♗xe5 Ï4xe5 30 ♘d2 ♘g6 31 ♘f3 Ïe4 32 h3 h6 33 Ïcc3 ♘e7 34 Ïd7 ♘f5 35 ♘d2 Ï4e6

35...Ïxe3 36 Ïxe3 Ïxe3 37 Ïxa7 gives White counterplay; 38 g4 is the immediate threat.

36 Ïcd3

36 ♘f1 ♘d6 37 ♘d2 Ïf8+ 38 ♔e2 Ïf7 expels White's rook from the seventh rank, leaving him no counterplay as the black king closes in on his weaknesses.

36...♘xe3 37 Ïxa7 ♘d1+!

Karpov makes beautiful use of his limited forces to generate a decisive attack.

38 ♔g1

38 ♔g3 (38 ♔f1? Ïe1#) 38...Ïg6+ 39 ♔f3 (39 ♔h2 Ïe2) 39...Ïf8+ 40 ♔e2 ♘b2 41 Ïdd7 Ïxg2+ gives White no real compensation for the pawn.

38...Ïg6 39 ♘f3

39 g4 Ïf6! harasses the white king, e.g. 40 Ïdd7 Ïe1+ 41 ♔h2 Ïe3 42 ♘e4 (42 Ïxg7+ ♔f8 wins, as there is no defence to 43...Ïf2+ and 44...Ïe1+) 42...Ïxe4 43 Ïxd1 Ïxc4 with a winning ending.

39...♘e3 40 ♘h4 Ïg5 41 Ïdd7 ♘xg2! 42 ♘f3

42 ♘xg2 Ïe2 is an excellent ending for Black, but now Karpov wins a second pawn.

42...Ïg6 43 ♔f2 ♘f4 44 Ïe7 ♘xh3+ 45 ♔e3 Ïe6+ 0-1

After the forced exchange of rooks, the black passed pawns will be unstoppable.

More Tactical Ideas

Deflection

Golubev-Kotov
Tula jr

Hopelessly behind on material, White got ready to leave, writing 'resigns' on his score-sheet, before folding and pocketing it. What was he trying to hide?

1...Ïxf7??

The future grandmaster falls for it! White really would have resigned after just about any other move.

2 ♗d8+! 1-0

Winning the queen (2...♔xd8 3 ♘xf7+), after which the ending is easy.

Golubev-Kotov is a good example of a combination based on deflection: if the bishop is taken, the king is lured away from the defence of his rook and on to the fatal d8-square.

The king is overloaded – he has two jobs to do but only one move! Deflection sacrifices are also made for positional ends, such as opening a line or unguarding an important square – see Babula-Blatny in the section on opposite bishops.

Back-Rank Mate

The castled king usually feels safest when the pawns in front have not been moved. However, once the rooks become active, there is a new danger: back-rank mate.

Bernstein-Capablanca
Moscow 1914

27 ♘xc3??

This capture looks like the logical conclusion of White's siege of the c-pawn, but he has overlooked the threat to his back rank. After 27 ♘d4 instead, there is everything to play for.

27...♘xc3 28 ♖xc3 ♖xc3 29 ♖xc3 ♕b2! 0-1

White loses at least a rook, for example: 30 ♕xb2 ♖d1#, 30 ♖c2

♕b1+ 31 ♕f1 ♕xc2, 30 ♕d3!? (hoping for 30...♖xd3?? 31 ♖c8+ mating) ♕a1+ 31 ♕f1 ♕xc3, or 30 ♕e1 ♕xc3!.

Crouch-Speelman
Hastings 1992

25...♖xa5??

25...♕xa5 is completely equal, e.g. 26 ♕xa5 ♖xa5 27 ♖xd7! ♖aa8. Now White missed the decisive...

26 ♖b8!

26 ♖xd7?? occurred in the game, which concluded peacefully after 26...♖f8 27 ♖b2 ♖xe5.

26...♖a8

26...♖xe5 27 ♖xd8# and 26...♖f8 27 ♕d6 lose at once.

27 ♖a1! ♕xa1

27...♖dxb8 28 ♖xa2 and Black cannot recapture.

28 ♖xd8+ (deflecting the rook) **28...♖xd8 29 ♕xa1** and the win is a matter of technique.

The best way to look after your back rank is to be alert, and make time to give your king an escape square before your opponent generates any serious threats.

Invasive Sacrifices

Few things give a chess player more pleasure than forcing checkmate by means of a devastating sacrificial combination. Rumour has it that Black's winning move in the next example so delighted the spectators that they showered the board with gold coins!

Lewitsky-Marshall
Breslau 1912

22...℟xh3!

22...℟g6 23 ♕e3 ♘f3+ 24 ♔h1 ♕xe5 wins an exchange, but this is stronger still.

23 ℟c5

Trying to complicate the game, since 23 gxh3 fails to 23...♘f3+ and 24...♘xg5.

23...♕g3!! 0-1

Not the only move, but certainly the strongest and most spectacular; 24 hxg3 ♘e2, 24 fxg3 ♘e2+ 25 ♔h1 ℟xf1 and 24 ♕e5 ♘f3+ 25 ♔h1 ℟xh2 are mate, while Black takes his extra piece into the ending after 24 ♕xg3 ♘e2+ 25 ♔h1 ♘xg3+ 26 ♔g1 (26 fxg3 ℟xf1#) 26...♘e2+ 27 ♔h1 ℟c3.

Another sacrifice on the same square. I like this even better since the idea could not be calculated completely and Kotov had to rely on his intuition when deciding to play it.

Averbakh-Kotov
Zurich Ct 1953

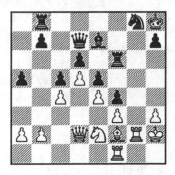

30...♕xh3+!!

An absolutely stunning move, one of the most famous in the history of chess. Black sacrifices his queen to drag the enemy king out to f5, where his own pieces, blocked in by the pawn chain, will be unable to save him.

31 ♔xh3 ℟h6+ 32 ♔g4 ♘f6+ 33 ♔f5

33 ♔g5 ℟h5#.

33...♘d7

This is the practical choice, but a quicker win was available with 33...♘g4!! (preventing the g2-rook from coming to the aid of its king) 34 ♘xf4 (34 fxg4 ♖f8#; 34 ♖xg4 ♖f8#; 34 ♔xg4 ♖g8+ 35 ♔f5 ♖f6#) 34...♖g8! (threatening 35...♖f6#) 35 ♘h5 ♖hg6! 36 ♕g5 (a regrettable necessity: the threat was 36...♖f8+ 37 ♘f6 ♖fxf6#) 36...♗xg5! 37 ♔xg4 (escaping the mating net, but at too high a price) 37...♗f4+ 38 ♔h3 ♖xg2 39 ♘xf4 exf4 and Black's extra exchange is decisive in the ending.

34 ♖g5!

White must defend against 34...♖f8+, 35...♖g8+ and 36...♖f6#.

34...♖f8+ 35 ♔g4 ♘f6+ 36 ♔f5 ♘g8+ 37 ♔g4 ♘f6+ 38 ♔f5 ♘xd5+

Black is repeating moves to gain time on the clock, but 37...♘g8+ 38 ♔g4 ♘f6+ is a draw by repetition. Taking the pawn on d5 changes the position, enabling him to extend the sequence of checks up to the time control at move 40.

39 ♔g4 ♘f6+ 40 ♔f5 ♘g8+ 41 ♔g4 ♘f6+ 42 ♔f5 ♘g8+ 43 ♔g4 ♗xg5 *(See next diagram)*

Kotov has had time to calculate the variations, and now moves in for the kill.

44 ♔xg5 ♖f7!

Averbakh has queen and bishop for rook and two pawns — a massive five 'points' ahead — but he still cannot save himself.

45 ♗h4

45 ♘xf4 ♖g7+ 46 ♘g6+ ♖gxg6+ 47 ♔f5 ♘e7#.

45...♖g6+ 46 ♔h5 ♖fg7 47 ♗g5 ♖xg5+ 48 ♔h4 ♘f6 49 ♘g3 ♖xg3 50 ♕xd6 ♖3g6 51 ♕b8+ ♖g8 0-1

White can only save his king by sacrificing his queen, leaving Kotov a whole piece up in the ending.

The Greek Gift

Polugaevsky-Tal
USSR Ch (Moscow) 1969

19 ♗xh7+!

This sacrifice, followed by ♘g5+ and queen to the h-file, constitutes the famous 'Greek Gift'. Although this is a fairly standard attacking mechanism, its success or failure can depend on the subtlest features of a position. Two themes which do recur are the white pawn on e5 – often required to chase the knight from f6 – and the insertion of h4 at some point, supporting the knight on g5.

19...♔xh7 20 ♘g5+ ♔g6

Black is forced to run the gauntlet, as 20...♔g8 21 ♕h4 is crushing, e.g. 21...♖e8 22 ♕h7+ ♔f8 23 e6! fxe6 (23...♖xe6 24 ♖xe6 fxe6 25 ♘xe6+) 24 ♕h8+ ♔e7 25 ♕xg7+ ♔d6 26 ♘f7+ winning the queen.

21 h4!! ♖c4

21...♘xd1 allows White to carry out his primary threat: 22 h5+ ♔xh5 23 g4+ ♔g6 24 ♕f5+ ♔h6 25 ♕h7+ ♔xg5 26 ♕h5+ ♔f4 27 ♕f5#; 21...f5 and 21...♕d7 ward off an immediate catastrophe, but 22 ♖d4! keeps the attack going, renewing the threat of 23 h5+.

22 h5+ ♔h6

22...♔xh5? walks into mate: 23 g4+ ♔g6 (23...♔h4 24 ♘f3+ ♔h3 25 ♕g3#; 23...♔h6 24 ♕h2+ ♔xg5 25 ♕h5+ ♔f4 26 ♕f5#) 24 ♕f5+ ♔h6 25 ♘xf7+ ♖xf7 26 ♕h5#.

· 23 ♘xf7+ ♔h7 24 ♕f5+ ♔g8 25 e6!

Incredibly, this position arose in Polugaevsky's preparation on the morning of the game!

25...♕f6 26 ♕xf6 gxf6 27 ♖d2 ♖c6

Now material equality is restored, but White's initiative persists into the endgame. The alternatives are worse.

28 ♖xb2 ♖e8 29 ♘h6+ ♔h7 30 ♘f5 ♖cxe6 31 ♖xe6 ♖xe6 32 ♖c2

Threatening 33 ♖c7+.

32...♖c6 33 ♖e2! ♗c8 34 ♖e7+ ♔h8 35 ♘h4 f5 36 ♘g6+ ♔g8 37 ♖xa7 1-0

Black cannot avoid further losses, e.g. 37...♖e6 (38 ♘e7+ was threatened) 38 ♖a8 ♖e8 39 ♖xc8! ♖xc8 40 ♘e7+, or 37...♖c1+ 38 ♔h2 ♗e6 39 h6 ♗f7 (the only defence to 40 ♖g7#) 40 h7+! ♔xh7 41 ♘e5 and the bishop is lost.

Trapping Pieces

Wedberg-Kharlov
Haninge 1992

9 ♗b3 b5!

Threatening simply 10...c4, trapping the bishop.

10 exd5 exd5 11 0-0

11 ♘xb5 ♕a5+ 12 ♘c3 used to be recommended as a good piece sacrifice for White, who gets a strong attack after 12...d4 13 0-0. However, 12...c4!

13 dxc4 dxc4 (13...d4!? deserves attention, now that the a2-g8 diagonal is closed) 14 ♗xc4 ♗xc3+ 15 ♗d2 (15 bxc3 ♕xc3+ 16 ♗d2 ♕xc4 is even worse for White) 15...♗xd2+ 16 ♕xd2 ♕xd2+ 17 ♔xd2 left White very short on compensation in Su-dan-Gallagher, Geneva 1993.

11...c4 12 dxc4 dxc4 13 ♕xd8+ ♘xd8!

13...♔xd8 14 ♘xb5 cxb3 15 axb3 gives White a lot of play against the 'active' black king, with ideas of ♗f4 and ♘g5 looming.

14 ♘xb5 cxb3 15 ♘c7+ ♔d7 16 ♘xa8 bxc2!

White is nominally the exchange ahead, but now another of his pieces is trapped – the knight on a8.

17 ♗f4

17 ♖f2 was Kharlov's suggested improvement, but one can only speculate that he was trying to fool potential opponents, since 17...♗b7 18 ♖d2+ ♘d5! is clearly better for Black.

17...♖f8! 18 ♘e5+ ♗xe5! 19 ♗xe5 ♖xf1+ 20 ♖xf1 ♘dc6 21 ♗c3 ♗a6 22 ♖c1 ♗d3 23 ♔f2 ♘d5 24 ♗d2 ♘cb4 25 a3

An unpleasant necessity; now the b3-square beckons the black knights.

25...♘c6 26 ♖e1 ♗f5 27 h3 h5 28 ♔g3 ♘d4 29 ♔h4 ♘b3 30 ♗g5 ♗d3 31 ♔g3 ♘c5 32 ♔f3 ♘e6 33 ♗c1 h4 34 ♔f2 ♗f5 35 g3 ♘c5 36 ♔f3 ♘d3 37 ♖g1 ♘xc1 38 ♖xc1 hxg3 39 ♔xg3 ♘e3 0-1

Black threatens 40...♘d1, when he either removes White's queenside pawns or (after b4) smokes the rook out with ...♘c3-a2. Meanwhile the knight on a8 is still not going anywhere, and can be rounded up at will.

Winning on Material

If you succeed in gaining a material advantage, the golden rule is this: exchange pieces! A material advantage becomes more valuable the fewer the pieces that remain. However, do not chase your opponent's pieces around on the off-chance that he will fall in with your plans, but play good positional moves and take your chances where you find them. For example, if you seize an open file with both rooks, the chances are your opponent will *have* to exchange pieces, rather than allow you to invade the seventh rank.

It has been said that the hardest thing in chess is winning a won game. This is not strictly true – winning a lost game usually poses more problems – but the point is that a moment's complacency can ruin a winning position.

Inexperienced players often use a material advantage as an excuse to start playing for a flashy attack or the win of even more material, regardless of whether or not the position justifies it. However eager you may be to force a quick decision, it is more important to win with as little risk as possible. Your opponent is more likely to resign if you keep control of the position than if you give him chances to fish in muddy waters.

5 The Opening

There are three principal objectives of opening play. The first is to move your pieces to effective positions as quickly as possible; this process is called development. The second is to fight for the central squares, the most important area of the board. The third is to prepare for the middlegame. This may sound trivial, but the transition from one phase of a game to the next is one of the most important, and most difficult, aspects of the game.

Development

In an ideal world, you would achieve perfect development every time by following the simple recipe below.

1. Occupy the centre with pawns; only make pawn moves that assist development.

2. Move knights and bishops towards the centre.

3. Move each piece once and once only, other than to make or avoid captures.

4. Castle into safety.

5. Move the queen to the second or third rank.

6. Clear the back rank to connect the rooks.

7. Place the rooks on open or semi-open files; if there are none, move them to the files most likely to be opened (usually those in or near the centre).

The importance of these principles may be gauged by applying them to the famous game below. The numbers in brackets after each move correspond to the rules being followed; these are italicised if the rule is broken.

Morphy-Count Isouard and Duke of Brunswick
Paris 1858

1 e4 (1) e5 (1) 2 ♘f3 (2) d6 (1) 3 d4 (1) ♗g4 (2)

A common piece of advice is 'Knights before bishops', and it is true that 3...♘f6 is an improvement here. The proverb, however, hints at the truth rather than states it. The point is that a knight on its original square has at most three legal moves, so its best square will usually be apparent early on. The bishop, by contrast, is at the mercy of the pawn formation – it may be some time before he knows where to find a good diagonal. This leads us to a much more useful rule:

In the opening, play moves that are necessary before moves that fit only some of the possibilities.

4 dxe5 (1) (3) ♗xf3 (*3*)

This second bishop move is the unhappy consequence of the first, since the natural 4...dxe5 loses a pawn after 5 ♕xd8+ ♚xd8 6 ♘xe5. Black not only concedes the bishop pair in an open position, but also exchanges his only developed piece. Meanwhile, White's lead in development increases, as he can recapture with a developing move.

5 ♕xf3 (5) dxe5 (1) 6 ♗c4 (2) ♘f6 (2)

This follows the rules but misses a tactic. 6...♕d7 is his best chance to hang on.

7 ♕b3 (3)

Morphy's second queen move is quite correct, as it gains time by threatening both b7 and f7.

7...♕e7 (2) (4) (5)

This move was intended to exchange queens after 8 ♕xb7 ♕b4+; however, the queen blocks in the bishop, which in turn prevents castling. Morphy rightly snubs the pawn and continues to develop.

8 ♘c3 (2) c6 (1) 9 ♗g5 (2) b5 (1)

White has won the opening: he is 4-2 ahead in development, and ready to castle on either side, while Black's hapless monarch is stranded in the centre. This adds up to a decisive attack, *but he must strike while the iron is hot*. A meek retreat such as 10 ♗e2 would give Black precious time to untangle his pieces.

10 ♘xb5! cxb5 11 ♗xb5+ ♘bd7 12 0-0-0

Both black knights are now pinned, and his king no nearer to castling.

12...♖d8 13 ♖xd7!

This exchanging combination is worth remembering: the attacking rook on d1 is replaced by its partner, but the defending rook is lured into the pin. Worse still, Black's reinforcements are trapped in the corner by his own pieces!

13...♖xd7 14 ♖d1 ♕e6 15 ♗xd7+ ♘xd7 16 ♕b8+! ♘xb8 17 ♖d8#

Entering the Middlegame

You've developed your pieces, castled into safety, and claimed a share of the centre. Your opponent also has done everything by the book, avoiding any serious positional concessions into the bargain. So what do you do now?

It's a common problem, but one largely neglected in chess literature. At the end of the opening, step back from move-by-move calculations, and formulate a general plan. Look at the pawn structure: which pawn breaks would either side like to play, how could the pawn structure change, who would have the advantage in an endgame? How are your pieces placed to deal with the possible transformations of the pawn structure? Which pieces aren't pulling their weight, where would you like them to be, and how will you get them there? What will your opponent do in the meantime?

Here are a couple of excellent examples of redeploying pieces.

Korchnoi-Fischer
Herceg-Novi blitz 1970

24...♘h8! 25 ♖d3 ♘f7 26 ♗f3
♘g5 27 ♕e2 ♖g6 28 ♔f1 ♘xh3 29
gxh3 ♗xh3+ 30 ♔f2 ♘g4+ 31
♗xg4 ♗xg4 0-1

Yusupov-Nogueiras
Montpellier Ct 1985

14 ♕d4!
Yusupov centralises his queen
which was offside and possibly vulnerable to an attack from the bishop
on d7.
14...f6

14...♕b6 15 e6 ♗xe6 16 ♕xg7.
15 exf6 gxf6 16 ♗xf6 ♖g8
16...♘xf6 17 ♕xf6 ♖g8 18 ♘xd5
♕xf6 19 ♘xf6+.
17 ♘b5! ♕xb5
17...♕xd4 18 ♘d6#.
**18 ♗xb5 ♘e6 19 ♕b2 cxb5 20
♗h4 1-0**

A fertile area for further study is
that of planning in the middlegame
and familiarising yourself with the
strategic ideas that fit the openings
and the pawn structures that arise.
Each pawn structure lends itself to
certain standard plans for both sides.
Once you have decided which openings you are going to play, study lots
of master games in your chosen
openings, preferably annotated, and
get a feel for where you should be
putting your pieces. A detailed study
of middlegame plans is beyond the
scope of this book, and I must refer
you to the Recommended Reading
section in Chapter 8.

6 So You Want to be a Grandmaster?

Well, you probably don't; the path to Grandmasterdom is a long and painful one. I can speak from bitter experience because I am still on it. I started playing chess when I was three years and eventually made it to International Master. I have been unable to surmount the final hurdle although I have not given up all hope yet. Unless you are extraordinarily talented, being a chess professional just does not pay. A glance at a top-class tournament taking place now (August 1995) sees 30 professional players fighting over a prize fund of about £3000 and each will play about 40 hours of chess. That works out at £2.50 per hour even before preparation, travel and ten nights' accommodation and food have been deducted. Clearly this band of professionals are running at a loss at this event. So I am not recommending chess as a career option but as a hobby it's guaranteed to give hours of pleasure. If you have absorbed some or even most of the instruction in this book you are well prepared to enter the world of organised chess. Alternatively you now have a huge advantage over the casual unschooled player and can probably beat all your friends! An estimated 3 million people have chess sets in their homes so finding an opponent is not too difficult. So where is chess actually played in this country?

Chess Clubs
Your first step to chess mastery, or just to finding some new opponents, should be to join a chess club; call your national federation or the London Chess Centre for details of clubs in your area. Don't imagine that you have to be an expert before daring to show your face – social players easily outnumber the chess wizards in most clubs. The 1993 Kasparov-Short match raised the profile of chess in Britain, and clubs around the country have benefited with increased memberships. A chess club will run internal competitions – typically a club championship, knockout and quickplay tournaments – and enter teams in local leagues. Most leagues operate numerous divisions, so that players of all standards can enjoy competitive chess at an appropriate level. Most clubs meet once a week and a few have a junior section.

Chess all day and night

What a lovely thought, but sadly there are very few venues in the UK where you can play anytime. Hastings and Edinburgh have chess clubs open seven days a week but there are precious few chess cafes or pubs. The chess players were recently removed from the King's Head Pub in West London where speed chess was formerly played every night. A recent innovation are the all-night blitz tournaments in Golders Green, North London. The only way to find an opponent 24 hours a day is on the Internet – see the next chapter.

Competitive Chess

Congresses

Every weekend throughout the year there are several weekend congresses held around the country. Typically they are divided into three sections: Open, Major and Minor. You should start off in the Minor until you play enough games to get a British Chess Federation grade which will indicate which section you should enter. Most congresses have five or six rounds. Some have a round on Friday evening and some make you play three games on a Saturday which can be quite exhausting. However, most allow you to take a half point bye and miss any round except the last one when the distribution of prize money is decided. Entry fees are generally between £10-£20.

One Day Quickplays

These are held on Saturday or Sunday and usually involve five or six games with half an hour on the clock for each player. Quickplay chess has slightly different rules so check up on these before you start play. Entry fees are usually around £10. Your national federation can provide you with a list of tournaments but the most up-to-date listings in the UK are to be found on Teletext page 478 and *Chess Monthly* magazine.

Swiss Tournaments

Almost all the weekend and one-day quickplay tournaments that take place around the country are run according to the Swiss system The Swiss system is based on the principle that players on the same score are paired together – as in all chess competitions, the scoring system is 1 point for a win, ½ for a draw and 0 for a defeat. Players are seeded according to grade or rating, and within each score group those seeded in the top half play those in the bottom half. Provided that there are enough rounds, it is impossible for more than one player to score maximum points. In this respect it resembles a knockout, but here the similarity ends. Nobody is eliminated under the Swiss system, and it is quite possible to come back from a bad start to win the tournament. Moreover, a slow starter will almost certainly meet lower-rated opposition than someone who leads from the front. A variation on this theme is the Accelerated Swiss, which is normally used for the larger international opens. The most distinctive feature of the Accelerated Swiss is that, in the early rounds, low-rated players who have started strongly meet high-rated players on a **lower** score. This maximises the norm opportunities for in-form players, by letting them loose on masters who may be struggling to get into gear.

The Swiss system rewards players who can make a very high percentage score against weaker opposition. It therefore encourages aggressive and uncompromising play, and a reduction in drawn games. On the minus side, mismatches where one player is heavily outgraded are common, and chances to meet players of one's own strength are limited.

National Competitions

A recent initiative is the Four Nations Chess League (4NCL), which at the time of writing has just completed its second season. The 4NCL is modelled on the semi-professional chess leagues that have existed in many European countries, notably Germany and France, for some years. Chris Dunworth, the 4NCL's organisational dynamo, aims to develop a competitive framework for club chess in Britain, similar to that which football has enjoyed for over a century. The 4NCL is intended as a catalyst for chess clubs to attract local sponsorship, and develop greater professionalism in the game.

If the 4NCL is the Premier League of chess, then the National Club Championship, organised by the British Chess Federation, is the F.A. Cup. Apart from the cash incentive, the prize for success is a place in the European Club Cup, and the chance to meet crack teams from Europe and the former USSR. A measure of the prestige of this competition is the fact that Kasparov himself played top board for the 1994 joint winners, Bosna Sarajevo in a gesture of solidarity.

My own team Wood Green from North London have played European team chess three times and became the first British club ever to win a match. The 4NCL aside, English clubs are exclusively amateur and do not have the resources to pay the top professionals to play. Consequently they were usually eliminated in the first round by teams from France, Germany or Eastern Europe where a professional team backed by local sponsorship is the norm. Wood Green were always outgraded by their opponents but managed to defeat teams from Denmark and Yugoslavia although we were crushed by Tel Aviv and a team of Grandmasters from Siberia who brought their own vodka!

Junior Chess

In recent years, four British players have struck gold at the World Junior Championships: Dharshan Kumaran (1991, under-16s), Luke McShane

(1992, under-10s), Ruth Sheldon (1993, under-14 girls) and Karl Mah (1994, under-14s). Luke drew with his first Grandmaster at the age of ten, and a year later has broken Nigel Short's record as the youngest player to qualify for the British Championship. He has also won several games aainst strong International Masters.

Organisers of junior events around the country keep a close eye on young players' results, inviting the most promising to join the BCF Junior Squad. This arranges championships in all age groups from under-7s to under-21s, coaching from master players, and opportunities to compete in major tournaments at home and abroad. The BCF's junior network relies exclusively on local volunteers but the system is extraordinarily successful with more fine young players emerging every year. I would like to pay tribute to the pioneering work done by Leonard Barden and Bob Wade, who 'discovered' many of today's grandmasters in the 1970s.

Schools Chess

The educational benefits of chess are hard to deny – concentration, memory and logical thinking to name but three – and schools are increasingly hiring top players to pass on their skills. Research carried out in schools in New Jersey found that chess is seriously good for your children. Unfortunately we have yet to see chess on the curriculum – the chess activity in any school really depends on the enthusiasm of a teacher working largely in his or her spare time. The Association of Chess Tutors and the London Chess Centre can organise professional coaching for any school that would like to develop chess but lacks the know-how. I have high hopes for a new project backed by Intel, the sponsors of the Professional Chess Association. Intel aim to get an extra 500 school chess clubs started this year with a cheap starter pack that includes sets, boards and a manual for teachers written by *Daily Telegraph* Weekend Correspondent David Norwood. There will also be a national schools competition that costs just 50p per child to enter. To join, contact the Intel Schools Chess Programme – details at the end of the chapter.

Knockout Tournaments

While the knockout is almost universal in tennis, it has been generally neglected in chess between London 1851 and some recent editions of the Tilburg and Wijk aan Zee tournaments in Holland. This may be because the cost of a single mistake in chess is generally much higher than in tennis, so players are reluctant to take risks, leading to dull games and a lot of draws – the exact opposite of what chess fans want to see.

The PCA/Intel Grand Prix may show the way forward for knockout chess. The PCA format consists of two game mini-matches (four in the final) played at a rate of 25 minutes per player per game, with a sudden-death tie break.

This is a blitz game, where White has an extra minute on the clock, but Black needs only a draw to go through. The faster time limit forces mistakes from the players, but produces dramatic games for the spectators.

Chess Clocks

All competitive chess is timed with a chess clock. The 1861 Anderssen-Kolisch match in London is the first known occasion on which chess was played to a time limit. An hourglass for each player was used to enforce a rate of 24 moves in two hours – soporific by today's standards, but supersonic compared to the stupefying deliberations of Elijah Williams, who would often spend upwards of two hours pondering his move. The book of the London 1851 tournament captures the atmosphere of his game with one James Mucklow admirably: 'Both players nearly asleep'.

The contemporary chess clock consists of two clocks linked together and operated by push buttons. When a player has made his move, he presses his button, stopping his own clock and starting his opponent's. Each clock has a small flag, which the minute hand picks up at about three minutes to the hour, and drops when the hour is completed.

A recent innovation is the digital clock. This has the advantage of showing exactly how much time remains in the crucial final minutes, and is more versatile than traditional clocks. For example, it can be set to 'Fischer mode', in which it counts down time in the usual way, but **adds** time whenever a move is made. The idea is to protect players from themselves, rationing their time to make sure they always have enough to avoid making grisly time-trouble blunders.

The table below shows the time limits commonly used in different kinds of tournament.

International	40 moves in 2 hours; 20 in 1 hour; remainder in 1 hour
Weekend	36 moves in 90 minutes; remainder in 15 minutes
Quickplay	30 minutes for all moves
Blitz	5 minutes for all moves
1 minute	Just move; don't think.
Lightning	Move at 10-second intervals

Adjournment and Adjudication

The trend in recent years has been to speed up time limits and complete games in a single session; however, adjournments and adjudications persist, especially in club chess. If a game is being adjourned, the player to move at the end of the session does not make his move on the board. Instead, he writes it on his score-sheet and puts it in an envelope, which is then sealed. Once the envelope is sealed, his move is completed and his clock stopped; details of the position and clock times are written on the envelope. When the game is resumed, the envelope is opened, the sealed move made on the board and play continues as normal.

If you have to seal a move, make absolutely sure that it is legal, legible and unambiguous – otherwise you will lose the game automatically. Also spare a thought for the Bulgarian GM Tringov, playing Korchnoi in the 1972 Olympiad, who sealed in an equal position. Both players analysed into the small hours, but on resumption the envelope was found to contain...nothing. Tringov forfeited the game, and Bulgaria lost the match 2½-1½. He later found the score-sheet in his jacket pocket!

Adjudication is a regrettable practice which persists in some local leagues. At the end of the playing session – which may be as early as move 30 – the players attempt to agree on a result. If this proves impossible, the game position is sent to a panel of experts who try to decide how the game would have turned out with best play from both sides.

Practical Tips and Tournament Etiquette

Offering a Draw

The correct time to offer a draw is straight after you make your move. If you offer a draw before moving, your opponent is entitled to see your move before making any decision. It is considered bad manners to offer a draw if it is not your move, if your opponent has already declined a draw or if you have a poor position.

Claiming a Draw

The procedure for claiming a draw by threefold repetition is as follows: write the intended move on your scoresheet, **but do not play it**. State your claim and call the arbiter (the tournament referee) to verify it. This may sound petty, but making the move on the board will invalidate your claim. A claim of a draw by repetition or 50 move rule must also be supported by a complete and correct record of the game to be considered. You may suffer a time penalty if you claim a draw wrongly.

Clock Handling

If you get too short of time to write down your moves, don't rely on your opponent's score-sheet – some unscrupulous characters will add a spurious move or two to deceive you. When you believe you have reached the time control, you must bring your score-sheet up to date. This is done with your clock running; turning out to be a move short having allowed your flag to fall is an occupational hazard. If neither player has a complete score when a flag falls, the clocks are stopped. Before the game can continue, the players must reconstruct the game on another board to see if a loss on time has occurred.

Remember if the time limit is 40 moves in two hour you must make 40 moves before your flag, countless numbers of games are lost when the flag falls with a player in the process of making his 40th move.

Bad Form

It is considered bad manners to eat or drink at the board, to stare at the opponent or distract him in any way. Nigel Short recently had to ask Gata Kamsky to stop coughing during the game. This so infuriated Gata's father Rustam that he later threw a huge tantrum and threatened to kill the then England No. 1. In fact he should have directed his request through the arbiter but in club chess a look should suffice to demonstrate one's displeasure.

British Chess Federations

The organisational structure of chess in the UK is a little confusing. The British Chess Federation (BCF) is really the English administration; the Scottish Chess Association was founded in 1884, 20 years earlier than the BCF; both the SCA and the Welsh Chess Union are fully autonomous bodies. The Irish Chess Union unites North and South, and even the Channel Islands have their own chess federation. However, major domestic events such as the British Championships, where all the above federations are represented, are organised by the BCF.

Grades, Ratings and Titles

Grades

Every year, the BCF publishes its grading list, which records the performance over the previous season of every active chess player in the country. It is easy to calculate your grade: for each game played, take the opponent's grade and add 50 points for a win, nothing for a draw, or deduct 50 for a defeat. Then add up your total score and divide by the number of games played – the resulting number is your grade.

The table below should not be taken as defining the named categories, but it gives a rough idea of the numbers involved:

Grandmaster	238+
International Master	225-237
FIDE Master	210-224
County player	175-209
Good club player	140-174
Average club player	100-139
Keen social player	60-99
Casual player	0-59

There is no theoretical maximum or minimum grade, but you may be interested to know that Grandmaster John Nunn topped the 1993-94 list at 259; the average of all graded players was 122.

The BCF grading system is simple, but rather slow-moving. The English chess season runs from May 1st to April 30th, but the grading list does not appear until the beginning of August. This means that a newcomer to chess may have over a year to wait before his results filter through to the grading list – long enough to test anyone's patience. Even worse, anyone whose chess shows a marked improvement over the season will be 'rewarded' with a grade well below his true playing strength, and then stuck with it for a whole year! The obvious solution is more regular grading lists and a shorter time lag; we can but hope.

International Ratings

FIDE publishes its international rating list on January 1st and July 1st each year, covering the periods June-November and December-May respectively. The minimum rating for inclusion is 2005.

The FIDE ratings are calculated using the system designed by Arpad Elo, a physics professor and nine-time chess champion of Wisconsin. There is no theoretical upper limit; the record for the highest FIDE rating is held by Kasparov at 2805.

To qualify for a FIDE rating, an unrated player must play at least 9 rated games at a performance level of at least 2005.

To convert a BCF grade to Elo, simply multiply by 8 and add 600.

The United States Chess Federation uses a system based on the Elo system. Every member of the USCF receives a free of the magazine *Chess Life* each month, with an updated rating on the mailing label.

Titles

FIDE awards international titles to players who have achieved a certain rating and scored two or three results of the requisite standard in tournament play. There are parallel schemes for men and women; however, it is debatable whether pitching women's titles 200 rating points below the men's encourages women to play more chess, or to settle for lower standards. Judit Polgar for one has shown how much she needs such 'positive discrimination': aged 15, she became the youngest ever GM, breaking the record Bobby Fischer held for 33 years.

At St. Petersburg 1914, the Czar suggested that the five leading players there – Lasker, Capablanca, Alekhine, Tarrasch and Marshall – should be considered the Grandmasters of chess. Since then, the number of strong players has mushroomed, and the number of IMs and GMs is well into four figures. It may surprise you to learn that the country with the highest concentration of GMs in its population is not Russia but Iceland!

Chess Politics

Whole books could be written about this but the last couple of years have seen some startling new and I believe positive developments, in particular the formation of the Professional Chess Association by Garry Kasparov and Nigel Short which aims to professionalise chess at the top level. Currently we have two world championship cycles which has confused many people so here is a brief summary of how it came about and where it might end.

FIDE versus PCA

The governing body of world chess is the Fédération Internationale des Echecs, better known by its acronym, FIDE (pronounced fee-day). Originally formed at the 1924 Paris Olympics by delegates from 15 countries, FIDE now boasts more member states than any other sporting organisation, bar FIFA (the corresponding body for soccer).

FIDE's first move was to launch a world team championship, known as the Olympiad, and a women's world championship tournament. First contested at London 1927, these were held concurrently and took place every other year until 1939. However, the real world championship was treated as the personal property of its holder from its inception in 1886 until 1946, when Alekhine died in possession. This was the turning point for FIDE, as it assumed responsibility for determining his successor, and simultaneously achieved full credibility with the affiliation of the USSR.

The new world championship comprised a three-year cycle, open to all. The cycle started with Zonal tournaments all over the world, leading to an Interzonal. The stars of the Interzonal, plus some seeded players, contested a Candidates tournament for the right to play a 24-game match with the reigning champion. This system was presumably conceived to ensure that the best player would win; however, it gives the champion such an advantage over his challengers as to defeat even this object. Other sports are perfectly happy to award their world title on the basis of a single tournament, often held annually, and such events tend to be more exciting and accessible for press and public alike. Although FIDE has tinkered endlessly with its formula, it remains essentially unchanged to this day.

FIDE started to award international titles in 1950, introducing titles of International Grandmaster, International Master and International Woman Master. In the same year, the Olympiads resumed and the women's world championship was reorganised along the same lines as the men's. The women's title had been vacant since 1944, when the champion Vera Menchik was killed at home in London by a V1 missile.

FIDE first published an international rating list in 1970, using a modified version of the Elo system pioneered in the USA. This enabled FIDE to fix an objective standard for the award of its titles, which had previously been conferred on a discretionary basis. The Woman Grandmaster title was created in 1977; the lower titles of FIDE Master and Woman FIDE Master followed the next year.

The turbulent state of chess politics today can be traced back to the extraordinary decision of FIDE President Campomanes to terminate the first Karpov-Kasparov world title match before it had reached a result. Kasparov felt he had been robbed of victory, and declared war on Campomanes. Kasparov's first 'player power' initiative was the Grandmasters' Association (GMA), created in 1987. The GMA organised the World Cup, effectively a Grand Prix in which the top players competed in four tournaments out of six, each player's three best scores being added to give the Grand Prix totals.

Despite the success of the first cycle in 1988-9, the World Cup collapsed after one tournament of the second. Having extracted certain concessions, the GMA board had voted to make peace with FIDE, but Kasparov disagreed and withdrew his co-operation. Without Kasparov, there could be no World Cup; without the World Cup, the GMA had lost its raison d'être. The GMA staggered on, only to suffer another body blow in February 1993 with the resignation of its President, Nigel Short. The following day, it was announced that Short's forthcoming world title match with Kasparov would be staged by a new organisation, the Professional Chess Association (PCA).

The chess world was stunned. Three days previously, FIDE had declared that the match would take place in Manchester, the only city to submit a bid in accordance with its regulations. Short argued that he had not been consulted, and that the prize fund of £1.15 million was not enough. Kasparov was only too happy to grind his political axe with FIDE some more. The fact that Short had spent the previous few weeks baiting Kasparov with playground insults was forgotten. The hand of the ubiquitous Raymond Keene – Grandmaster, Channel 4 presenter, chess correspondent of *The Times*, renowned organiser of major chess events, defeated candidate for the FIDE vice-presidency – was clearly discernible in the background although nowadays he has no connection whatever with the PCA which is run by a board of five directors and has offices in New York run by Bob Rice, an American Corporate lawyer.

Scepticism about the fledgling organisation was rife, not least because the contact number on the momentous press release belonged to Keene's nanny! Did the PCA plan to benefit more than two or three people? Would Kasparov tell Short 'Thanks, but no thanks' if a match with, say, Anand proved more interesting to potential sponsors? Wasn't the PCA turning the clock back half a century by allowing the champion to make his own rules?

The doubters and the FIDE hierarchy were silenced by events. The PCA managed to raise the prize fund to £1.7 million, courtesy of *The Times*. Channel 4 bought exclusive TV rights, and screened two hours' coverage on playing days. Even Princess Diana turned up in the audience one day. The only black mark was the organisation of the match itself. At the outset *The Times* decided to price tickets at the ridiculous price of £80 and not surprisingly hardly any were sold. Game 1 looked like being an embarrassment and new organisers were hired and the previous ones fired. Ticket prices were slashed to £20 and there was even a special half price promotion in *The Sun*. A few days before the start of the match two of the organisers visited the London Chess Centre to hire some equipment and looked sheepish when I questioned them about ticket sales. I offered to fill the theatre for them on game 1 but they would have to give tickets away. *The Times* trumpeted game 1 as a sell-out but in fact it was a give-out. I personally gave away 100s of tickets and made lots of new friends. Nevertheless, the match gave chess in Britain a huge boost and Channel 4 were delighted with viewing figures that exceeded anything they had ever achieved in the same time slots. Meanwhile, FIDE's 'official' world championship match between Karpov and Timman was lurching from one crisis to another.

The opening ceremony witnessed the mayor of Zwolle innocently delivering his speech while the backdrop behind him burst into flames. The Dutch hosts of the first half failed to raise a single guilder in prize money. Oman withdrew its support for the second half, ostensibly because of the economic recession but in reality because they had never actually given their written agreement or a bank guarantee. Now the FIDE protagonists were playing for nothing! However, Campomanes' ability to pull rabbits from his hat is legendary, and he did not disappoint. A new backer was found in Indonesia, the match was completed and the players got paid – reputedly at the personal expense of the FIDE board members.

FIDE retaliated by stripping Kasparov and Short of their ratings, a move which only diminished the integrity of its rating system. The PCA produced its own rating list, organised its own world championship cycle, and announced a massive sponsorship deal with Intel. The manufacturers of the Pentium processor received an unexpected return on their investment, when it defeated Kasparov himself in the London leg of the 1994 PCA/Intel Grand Prix.

Disaster struck FIDE once more in September 1994: the Thessaloniki Olympiad, scheduled for December, was cancelled after the Greek government failed to confirm its sponsorship commitments. Nevertheless, FIDE was bailed out by a most unexpected ally ... the pro-Kasparov Russian Chess Federation offered to host the Olympiad in Moscow! This organisation, incidentally, was fighting an acrimonious battle for supremacy over the 'official' Russian federation – the legitimate offspring of the former USSR Chess Federation – backed by Karpov.

The sight of Kasparov getting into bed with his sworn enemy astounded most people, but not Timman. He pointed out that Kasparov had sought reconciliation with Campomanes twice before, on the occasion of the last two FIDE presidential elections; this time the President needed the World Champion. There was only one small problem the FIDE constitution prevented Campomanes from contesting the election, not having announced his intention to stand in time. The irrepressible Campo persuaded the delegates to vote for a change in the regulations, whereupon his re-election for a fourth term on a platform of co-operation with the PCA was a formality.

Now that peace has broken out, it may be that the two-tier system advocated by Kasparov will become a reality: the PCA running top-level events including the world championship, FIDE responsible for the Olympiad and amateur chess. Kasparov and Short have been reinstated on the FIDE rating list, which has not, however, accounted for their games or PCA events in the intervening period. Finally, a reunification match is planned for 1996, between the PCA and FIDE champions. However, FIDE appears to have sold out Karpov, accepting Kasparov's condition that the FIDE champion will have the status of challenger in this match. FIDE has also been unable to find a sponsor for their final between Karpov and Kamsky principally because in the eyes of the world Kasparov is the true World Champion.

7   A Brief History of Chess

Board Games and Fortune-Telling
The pre-history of chess is a fertile area for speculation due to the scarcity of hard evidence. Board games have been played for at least 4000 years, but the earliest game recognisable as chess, chaturanga, is not documented before about 625 AD.

Chaturanga
Chaturanga is believed to have originated in north-west India in the period 606-620 AD. This narrow time-frame is the conclusion of Pavle Bidev, a Yugoslav professor of philosophy; if correct, it suggests that the transformation of the religious ceremony into Chaturanga may have been the work of an individual. Perhaps the defining moment of the 'invention' of chess was the elimination of the dice to produce a game of pure skill.

The word 'chaturanga' means 'having four parts' in Sanskrit, and also referred to a platoon in the contemporary Indian army, consisting of a chariot, an elephant, horses and foot-soldiers. A minister and a king were added to complete the war scenario. The 8x8 board was probably adopted from ashtapada, an ancient Indian race game played with dice. The word 'ashtapada' is Sanskrit for 'having eight legs', and was used variously for the game, the board, spiders, and a mythical eight-legged creature.

Legend has it that chaturanga was invented by a wise man, to show an arrogant Rajah that he could not win a battle without the help of his subjects. Delighted with the game, the Rajah offered the wise man anything he liked as a reward, but all he asked for was one grain of corn on the first square of the chessboard, two on the second, four on the third and so on, doubling the number of grains on each square up to the sixty-fourth. When it dawned on the Rajah that the number of grains needed was astronomical (over 18 billion billion), he had the wise man executed for his cheek!

Shatranj
Chaturanga reached Persia around 625, where it became known as Chatrang; it was renamed Shatranj after the Arab conquest of 638-651. The period from the 8th to 10th centuries is regarded as a Golden Age of Islamic chess, in which the opening and endgame were thoroughly investigated, and strategy became highly developed. The Caliphs themselves were avid players.

The opening in Shatranj was slow, the opposing forces taking a long time to come into contact. To cut down on preliminaries, a number of 'tabiya' positions were identified. These were common positions from the opening, typically arising between moves 8 and 20, which were considered to be roughly equal. Rather than start from the initial set-up, players would agree on a tabiya position and begin play from there.

Shatranj was known throughout Europe by about 1000. The journey west began in the 8th century with the Moorish invasion of Spain, followed shortly by the Islamic conquest of Sicily and the Byzantine Christians moving through the Balkans. The game penetrated Russia from all directions: by trade routes from the Caspian Sea up the Volga and from Byzantium to Kiev, by the Vikings from the Baltic, and directly from India via the Uzbeks.

Medieval Chess

The evolution of chess continued unabated in medieval Europe. The chequered board was in use by 1100. In the 12th century, the fers (minister) was granted an initial double move – a privilege also extended to a newly promoted fers. The Alfonso Manuscript of 1283 describes the pawn's double move, and around the same time Cessole recorded that a previously unmoved king could make a double move or even leap to b1 or b2. Stalemate had been downgraded to a draw by 1422, and the *en passant* rule was another 15th century innovation. These innovations were by no means universal, however, and there was a wide range of regional variations.

The most dramatic change occurred around 1475, when the aufin (elephant) and fers were upgraded to the bishop and queen we know today. Castling as a single move was introduced in the 16th century, in response to the increased attacking force available. Originally, 'free' castling was practised: the king could move any number of squares along the back rank towards the corner, while the rook could move as far as the e-file.

The modern rules slowly crystallised, as successive introductory manuals and, later, the leading chess clubs published their own sets of rules. Some anomalies persisted until surprisingly recently: stalemate was still counting as a win in London until 1807, while the Italians did not officially incorporate *en passant* or standardised castling until 1880.

The Top Twenty?

This selection includes the thirteen official World Champions to date, plus seven other leading players who have profoundly influenced the development of the game. It does not pretend to name the 'best' players of all time, however: any such comparison would be meaningless, as the general standard of play increases continually. As Kasparov said when asked to compare himself with Fischer, it's like comparing two generals from different eras: 'they were fighting with different weapons'. The discovery of one genius is common knowledge to the generations which follow.

Francois-André Danican Philidor (1726-95)

The young Philidor had a precocious talent for music, joining the Versailles Chapel-Royal choir aged 6, and composing a motet aged 11 which was performed for Louis XV. He went on to compose 25 comic operas, which were held in the highest regard by Parisian society. Philidor learned his chess at the Café de la Régence, where he took lessons from Legall, the strongest player of the day.

Philidor's *L'analyse des echecs*, still remembered for the motto 'Pawns are the soul of chess', was published in 1749. It explained for the first time the elements of positional play, in particular pawn structure and the centre. Prior to this, players would attack at any cost, unaware that the success of their venture depended on anything other than their own tactical ingenuity. Philidor was far ahead of his contemporaries, and rarely played on level terms. He regularly gave odds of 'pawn and move' – taking Black and playing without an f7-pawn – and astounded his contemporaries by playing, blindfold, up to three games simultaneously.

Count Bruehl-Philidor
London 1783

1 e4 e5 2 &c4 c6 3 ♕e2 d6 4 c3 f5 5 d3 ♘f6 6 exf5?

This is a mistake, giving up the important e4 point. Much better is 6 f4, keeping the tension and pressurising e5.

6...&xf5 7 d4 e4 8 &g5 d5 9 &b3 &d6 10 ♘d2 ♘bd7 11 h3 h6 12 &e3 ♕e7

Philidor appears to have anticipated Nimzowitsch's theory of overprotection: he concentrates as much force as possible on his strong-point, the head of the pawn chain at e4.

13 f4

This renounces all hope of the undermining move f3, and hands Black a protected passed pawn, which will be a great asset in any ending.

13...h5 14 c4 a6 15 cxd5 cxd5 16 ♕f2 0-0 17 ♘e2 b5 18 0-0 ♘b6 19 ♘g3 g6 20 ♖ac1 ♘c4 21 ♘xf5 gxf5

Naturally, Philidor has no objection to off-loading his bad bishop and consolidating his centre.

22 ♕g3+ ♕g7 23 ♕xg7+ ♔xg7 24 &xc4 bxc4 25 g3 ♖ab8

Black immediately seizes the half-open b-file, hitting the b2-pawn.

26 b3 &a3! 27 ♖c2 cxb3 28 axb3 ♖bc8

The crafty ...&a3 has deprived White of the c1-square for his rooks, so he must now concede the c-file.

29 ♖xc8 ♖xc8 30 ♖a1 &b4 31 ♖xa6 ♖c3

Philidor's pawn sacrifice is only temporary, as White is in no position to resist the rook's invasion. Now 33 ♗f2? fails to 33...e3 with a lethal fork.

32 ♔f2 ♖d3 33 ♖a2 ♗xd2 34 ♖xd2 ♖xb3

The 'tall pawn' on e3 is no match for Black's knight, with the position blocked and the pawns all on the same side of the board. With the e4-pawn dominating the position, Philidor has a decisive advantage.

35 ♖c2 h4! 36 ♖c7+ ♔g6 37 gxh4 ♘h5 38 ♖d7 ♘xf4 39 ♗xf4 ♖f3+ 40 ♔g2 ♖xf4 41 ♖xd5 ♖f3

The tactical sequence initiated by 35...h4 has given Black two connected passed pawns, which will be unstoppable when supported by the rook. Therefore it is neither necessary nor desirable to take on h4.

42 ♖d8 ♖d3 43 d5 f4 44 d6 ♖d2+ 45 ♔f1 ♔f7 46 h5 e3 47 h6 f3 0-1

48 ♔g1 ♖g2+ 49 ♔h1 e2 does nothing but delay the inevitable.

Adolf Anderssen (1818-79)

Anderssen's life outside chess was quite unremarkable. Never married, he lived quietly with his mother and taught mathematics at the Friedrichs Gymnasium in his home town of Breslau (now Wroclaw). In the chess world, however, he was renowned for his exceptional combinational vision. He won three major tournaments, including the first ever international tournament at London 1851, but it was an offhand game he played in the foyer of Simpson's-in-the-Strand, which maintains its

chess tradition to this day. It has become known as 'The Immortal Game'.

Anderssen-Kieseritzky
London 1851

1 e4 e5 2 f4 exf4 3 ♗c4 ♕h4+

It is tempting to deprive White of the right to castle, but the exposed position of the black queen is more significant. It is better to play for ...d5, either immediately (3...d5 4 ♗xd5 ♘f6), or after 3...♘f6 4 ♘c3 c6.

4 ♔f1 b5?

This just loses a pawn; Black's enthusiasm to open lines backfires, as his development is the more difficult.

5 ♗xb5 ♘f6 6 ♘f3 ♕h6 7 d3

Simply 7 ♘c3 intending d4 gives White a huge advantage.

7...♘h5

This is a highly dubious enterprise, neglecting development for the cheap threat 8...♘g3+, and if 8 ♔f2 or ♔g1, 8...♕b6+ picks up the bishop.

8 ♘h4 ♕g5 9 ♘f5 c6 10 g4!

This bold thrust seizes the initiative for White, who is not afraid to sacrifice a piece for a lead in development.

10...♘f6 11 ♖g1 cxb5 12 h4 ♕g6 13 h5 ♕g5 14 ♕f3

Now White threatens both 15 ♗xf4 trapping the queen, and 15 e5 regaining the piece with advantage.

14...♘g8 15 ♗xf4 ♕f6 16 ♘c3 ♗c5

A piece is a small price to pay for such an overwhelming position, but the game will not play itself. White must be resolute, and strike before the opponent organises his forces.

17 ♘d5!! ♕xb2 18 ♗d6

The rooks are not needed for the attack, so Anderssen sacrifices them!

18...♗xg1

18...♕xa1+ 19 ♔e2 ♕xg1 fails to 20 ♘xg7+ ♔d8 21 ♗c7#, and 18...♗xd6 to 19 ♘xd6+ ♔d8 20 ♘xf7+ ♔e8 21 ♘d6+ ♔d8 22 ♕f8#.

19 e5!

This charming quiet move blocks the queen's defence of g7, and threatens mate in two.

19...♕xa1+ 20 ♔e2 ♘a6

Black covers c7, but it is too little, too late. Anderssen crowns a fantastic game with a queen sacrifice to force mate.

21 ♘xg7+ ♔d8 22 ♕f6+! ♘xf6 23 ♗e7#

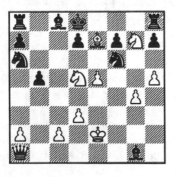

Black has an extra queen, bishop and two rooks scattered around the board, but nothing where it counts – defending his king.

Paul Morphy (1837-84)

The meteoric rise and subsequent burn-up of Morphy's chess career has earned him the tag 'the pride and sorrow of chess'. Between the ages of 8 and 13, he played regularly with the best in New Orleans, and overcame them all. He turned his attention to a more socially acceptable career in law, graduating in 1857 while he was still too young to practise. The next year he travelled to Europe, where he defeated Löwenthal, Harrwitz and Anderssen – respectively the champions of England, France and Germany – by huge margins. The only rival to elude him was Howard Staunton, probably the strongest player of the 1840s, who was by this time semi-retired from chess and committed to producing his edition of Shakespeare's plays to a tight schedule.

Morphy was the first American to conquer the Old World in any discipline, and returned home in 1859 to a hero's welcome. He commanded the extraordinary fee of $3000 to write a chess column in the *New York Ledger*, but the editor regarded him as 'incorrigibly lazy' and soon dispensed with his services. Morphy was alienated by the Civil War, in which he had no desire to participate, and failed as a lawyer. He ended his days a recluse, suffering increasingly from depression and paranoia.

Botvinnik summarised Morphy's contribution to chess as follows: 'Morphy remains the unsurpassed master of the open games ... since Morphy, nothing significantly new has been achieved in this field'.

Morphy-Anderssen
Paris 1858
1 e4 d5 2 exd5 ♕xd5 3 ♘c3 ♕a5 4 d4 e5?

It was Morphy who was first to understand that a lead in development increases in value the more open a position becomes. Black is impatient to release his pieces, but the calm 4...♘f6 intending 5...c6 is better.

5 dxe5 ♕xe5+ 6 ♗e2 ♗b4 7 ♘f3!

Naturally, Morphy has no objection to offering a pawn for the two bishops and free development.

7...♗xc3+ 8 bxc3 ♕xc3+ 9 ♗d2 ♕c5 10 ♖b1 ♘c6 11 0-0 ♘f6 12 ♗f4 0-0!

This is an excellent and thoroughly modern move. Anderssen refuses to be a martyr for his extra pawn, and minimises his disadvantage by returning it.

13 ♗xc7 ♘d4

13...♘d5! 14 ♖b5 ♕e7 (Karpov) also forces the exchange of the dark-squared bishop, but leaves Black with a more effective knight on c6.

14 ♕xd4 ♕xc7 15 ♗d3 ♗g4

This move runs into tactical problems, as the queen and knight are overloaded with the defence of b7, h7 and g4. But even after 15...h6 16 ♕e5! ♕xe5 17 ♘xe5 intending f4 and ♗c4, White has a clear advantage.

16 ♘g5! ♖fd8

16...♗h5 loses a pawn after 17 ♘e4 ♘xe4 18 ♕xe4 ♗g6 19 ♕xb7, but at least gives some chances of saving the endgame.

17 ♕b4

Threatening both 18 ♕xb7 and 18 ♘xh7 ♘xh7 19 ♕xg4.

17...♗c8 18 ♖fe1 a5 19 ♕e7

Seizing the seventh rank, as 19...♖d7? runs into 20 ♕e8+! and mate next move.

19...♕xe7 20 ♖xe7 ♘d5?!

Black could try 20...♖d7, when 21 ♖be1? ♖xe7 22 ♖xe7 h6! 23 ♘xf7?? loses a piece after 23...♔f8 24 ♖c7 ♘e8, but 21 ♖xd7 ♘xd7 22 ♗c4! wins a good pawn (22...♘e5? 23 ♖e1!).

21 ♗xh7+ ♔h8 22 ♖xf7 ♘c3 23 ♖e1 ♘xa2 24 ♖f4 ♖a6 25 ♗d3 1-0

Black cannot avoid heavy material losses.

Wilhelm Steinitz (1836-1900)

Steinitz was born in Prague but moved to Vienna as a young man, where he tried his luck as a journalist. After winning the Vienna championship in 1861-2, however, he moved to London and became a chess professional. Steinitz defeated Anderssen 8-6 (with no draws!) in 1866, but it was not until 1873 that he developed his theory of closed positions and departed from the gambit style of his contemporaries. Steinitz was an objective annotator of games both his own and other people's which he published in his column in *The Field*. Steinitz was unseated from *The Field* by Hoffer and moved to America where he produced the *International Chess Magazine* from 1885-1891 in which he propounded his theories.

An official World Championship match had to wait until after Morphy had died, Steinitz duly claiming the title with his victory over Zukertort in 1886. After losing his rematch with Lasker, Steinitz suffered a mental breakdown: among his delusions was the idea he could beat God at odds of pawn and move.

Steinitz's thesis was the accumulation of small, long-term, advantages. He would go to extreme lengths to avoid weakening his pawn structure, and gladly defend a cramped and difficult position in the pursuit of some eventual positional gain.

Siegbert Tarrasch (1862-1934)

Tarrasch achieved excellent tournament results over a long period, but missed his best chance to capture the world title. In 1893, he was playing as well as anyone, and might have challenged the ageing Steinitz but for the demands of his work as a general practitioner. Tarrasch was in the twilight of his career when he finally arranged a match with Lasker, which he lost decisively.

Today, Tarrasch is better remembered for his teachings on the game. It was he who distilled the genius of Steinitz, filtered out the eccentricities, and derived a set of general principles which the ordinary player could understand. He added a few personal touches, too: whereas Steinitz insisted above all on avoiding pawn weaknesses, Tarrasch valued active piece play more highly. His dogmatic, even mechanical, approach was criticised by some of his contemporaries, and not without reason; nevertheless, he was arguably closer than any of them to the 1990s conception of chess.

Nimzowitsch-Tarrasch
St Petersburg 1914

1 d4 d5 2 ♘f3 c5 3 c4 e6 4 e3 ♘f6 5 ♗d3 ♘c6 6 0-0 ♗d6 7 b3 0-0 8 ♗b2 b6 9 ♘bd2 ♗b7 10 ♖c1 ♕e7 11 cxd5

Positions where the pawn centre is in a state of tension are difficult to play, as every possible transformation of the structure has to be calculated. In general, however, resolving the tension without a good follow-up will rebound unfavourably, and in this case White should have been content with 11 ♕e2.

11...exd5 12 ♘h4 g6 13 ♘hf3 ♖ad8 14 dxc5 bxc5

Nimzowitsch has 'inflicted' hanging pawns on his opponent, but with no pieces yet exchanged, and Black well co-ordinated, these are a strength rather than a weakness.

15 ♗b5 ♘e4 16 ♗xc6 ♗xc6 17 ♕c2 ♘xd2 18 ♘xd2

18 ♕xd2 allows Black to break through with 18...d4! 19 exd4 ♗xf3 20 gxf3 ♕h4.

18...d4!
Anyway!
19 exd4 ♗xh2+!! 20 ♔xh2 ♕h4+ 21 ♔g1 ♗xg2!
There is no black knight to support the 'Greek gift' pattern here, so Tarrasch wades in with a classic double bishop sacrifice.
22 f3
22 ♔xg2 ♕g4+ 23 ♔h2 ♖d5 and swings over to give mate on the h-file.
22...♖fe8!
This excellent move, cutting off the king's escape on the e-file, is an essential part of the combination. Now 23...♖e2 is threatened, but 23 ♕d3 fails to 23...♕g3 24 ♘e4 ♖xe4 25 ♕xe4 ♗xf3+ winning the queen.
23 ♘e4 ♕h1+ 24 ♔f2 ♗xf1 25 d5
25 ♖xf1 ♕h2+; 25 ♘f6+ ♔f8 26 ♘xe8 ♕g2+.
25...f5 26 ♕c3
White generates a small threat, but unfortunately it is too late to save

his own king from being hunted to its death.
26...♕g2+ 27 ♔e3 ♖xe4+! 28 fxe4 f4+! 29 ♔xf4 ♖f8+ 30 ♔e5
30 ♔e3 ♕f2#.
30...♕h2+ 31 ♔e6 ♖e8+ 32 ♔d7 ♗b5# 0-1

Emanuel Lasker (1868-1941)

Lasker was world chess champion for 27 years, but had many other interests and talents: he also made a significant contribution to mathematics, and wrote books on philosophy, bridge (at which he represented Germany) and other games. Lasker's philosophical work sought to draw parallels between chess and the battles of everyday life, and his general theory of the struggle was the foundation of his uncompromising chess style.

Lasker won so many difficult positions that his fellow masters attributed him with almost supernatural powers. In truth, his success had nothing to do with witchcraft and a lot to do with his understanding of tension in chess – that is, the physical complexity of a position, not to be confused with the psychological tension which attends any sporting contest. Lasker's risky play created complicated situations demanding absolute accuracy from both sides: even if he stood worse in theory, time and again he would find more 'only moves' than his opponent and emerge victorious.

José Capablanca (1888-1942)

Capablanca was a child prodigy: at the age of four, he learned the moves from watching his father play, and promptly beat him twice! Aged 12, he defeated Corzo 7-5 for the Havana Chess Club championship, and at 21 thrashed Marshall, the US champion, 8-1 with 14 draws. Capablanca was only invited to San Sebastian 1911 at Marshall's insistence, but created a sensation by taking first prize ahead of all the world's best players, bar Lasker. He then challenged Lasker to a match for the supreme title, but negotiations broke down in a dispute over Lasker's conditions. In 1920, the ageing Lasker tried to abdicate quietly, but gave in to the public demand for a match; in the event, he resigned his title after going 4-0 behind.

Capablanca had phenomenal natural talent, and no taste for hard work. With the world title in the bag, and a playboy lifestyle afforded by his position as a Cuban ambassador, he presumably felt no need to change. He was regarded as a 'chess machine': moving quickly, finding the right plan intuitively, and very seldom losing a game. However, his over-confidence cost him the title when he failed to take Alekhine's challenge seriously. He was never granted a re-match.

This game fragment shows 'Capa' playing the 'Fischer endgame', discussed on page 42, reaching a favourable rook and pawn endgame and demonstrating how an active king and rook can more than compensate for a pawn.

Capablanca-Tartakower
New York 1924

27 h5! Rf6 28 hxg6 hxg6 29 Rh1 Kf8 30 Rh7 Rc6 31 g4! Nc4 32 g5! Ne3+ 33 Kf3 Nf5 34 Bxf5 gxf5 35 Kg3!! Rxc3+ 36 Kh4 Rf3 37 g6 Rxf4+ 38 Kg5 Re4 39 Kf6! Kg8 40 Rg7+ Kh8 41 Rxc7 Re8 42 Kxf5

The material has been regained and the piece positions transformed. Black is totally passive.

42...Re4 43 Kf6 Rf4+ 44 Ke5 Rg4 45 g7+ Kg8

45...Rxg7 46 Rxg7 Kxg7 47 Kxd5 Kf7 48 Kc6 Ke7 49 Kb7 Kd6 50 Kxa7 Kd5 51 Kxb6.

46 Rxa7 Rg1 47 Kxd5 Rc1 48 Kd6 Rc2 49 d5 Rc1 50 Rc7 Ra1 51 Kc6 Rxa4 52 d6 1-0

Alexander Alekhine (1892-1946)
The story of Alekhine's life has all the makings of a Hollywood movie. Born into a wealthy Russian family, he had the misfortune to be at a tournament in Mannheim when war broke out in 1914. He was interned by the Germans, but certified unfit for military service – allegedly feigning mental illness – and re-

leased. Alekhine returned to Russia, served on the Austrian front, and was twice wounded and twice decorated – but come the Revolution of 1917, his family lost everything and only his chess talent saved him from a worse fate.

Alekhine manoeuvred his way out of Russia in 1921, joining the Communist Party and marrying a Swiss Comintern delegate – neglecting to mention his existing marriage to a Russian baroness, and their young daughter. Alekhine settled in Paris, where he acquired a third wife and a self-styled 'doctorate', after writing half a thesis on the Chinese penal system. He was obsessed with chess, and developed his great talent with eight hours' study a day. Having secured the world title in 1927, Alekhine took care not to risk it against his strongest rivals; nevertheless, his taste for alcohol brought him a shock defeat in 1935. Euwe graciously agreed to a rematch; drinking nothing stronger than milk, Alekhine easily regained his title.

Botvinnik's challenge was accepted around June 1939, but the outbreak of war sunk this titanic match. Alekhine hurried to join the French army as an interpreter, and when France surrendered he sought asylum, first in Cuba and then in the USA. However, the authorities were not impressed by the series of anti-Semitic articles he had contributed to the Nazi press, and even his offer of a match to Capablanca fell on deaf ears.

Alekhine played in several Nazi-sponsored tournaments between 1941 and 1943, later claiming that his collaboration was the price of his (fourth) wife's liberty.

From 1943 onwards, ostracised by the allied powers, Alekhine drifted around Spain and Portugal earning a pittance from chess. However, the Communists' desire for the world title outweighed their ideological hostility to Alekhine himself, and Botvinnik's challenge was revived. The Moscow Chess Club had guaranteed the prize fund, and the British Chess Federation had agreed to host the match. Within hours of receiving confirmation, Alekhine died in his Lisbon boarding house.

Alekhine's play was characterised by energy, dynamism and long combinations with a 'sting in the tail', while his annotated games collections are classics of chess literature. In a curious footnote to the life history above, Alekhine was rehabilitated by the Communists in the 1950s, as they evidently decided he was too good a player not to claim as one of their own.

Réti-Alekhine
Baden-Baden 1925
1 g3 e5 2 ♘f3 e4 3 ♘d4 d5 4 d3 exd3 5 ♕xd3

Réti's choice of opening seems like some kind of private joke: he is playing Alekhine's Defence (1 e4 ♘f6) with colours reversed! However, this move is artificial, and the simple 5 cxd3 deserves preference.

5...♘f6 6 ♗g2 ♗b4+ 7 ♗d2 ♗xd2+ 8 ♘xd2 0-0 9 c4 ♘a6!?

Alekhine intends to make the most of the queen's exposed position.

10 cxd5 ♘b4 11 ♕c4 ♘bxd5 12 ♘2b3 c6 13 0-0 ♖e8 14 ♖fd1 ♗g4 15 ♖d2 ♕c8 16 ♘c5 ♗h3!

17 ♗f3

17 ♗xh3 ♕xh3 18 ♘xb7 ♘g4 19 ♘f3 ♘de3!! forces the win of the queen, e.g. 20 fxe3 ♘xe3 21 ♕xf7+ ♔h8 (of course not 21...♔xf7 22 ♘g5+ and 23 ♘xh3) 22 ♘h4 ♖f8 and if the queen leaves the f-file, 23...♖f1+ mates.

17...♗g4 18 ♗g2 ♗h3 19 ♗f3 ♗g4 20 ♗h1

A brave decision: White declines the draw by repetition with 20 ♗g2, and challenges Alekhine to a sharp struggle.

20...h5! 21 b4

A race now develops, with the players attacking on opposite sides of the board.

21...a6 22 ♖c1 h4 23 a4 hxg3 24 hxg3 ♕c7 25 b5

More prudent is 25 e4, throwing a spanner in the works before continuing his own attack.

25...axb5 26 axb5 ♖e3!?

27 ♘f3?

27 fxe3?? ♕xg3+ 28 ♗g2 ♘xe3 is crushing, but the cold-blooded 27 ♗g2! stops all the sacrifices and leaves Black struggling to find a follow-up. Réti's choice is natural enough, but allows Black to seize the initiative with a deep combination.

27...cxb5 28 ♕xb5 ♘c3 29 ♕xb7 ♕xb7 30 ♘xb7 ♘xe2+ 31 ♔h2

31 ♔f1 ♘xg3+ 32 fxg3 ♗xf3 33 ♗xf3 ♖xf3+ 34 ♔g2 ♖aa3 35 ♖d8+ ♔h7 36 ♖h1+ ♔g6 37 ♖h3 ♖fb3 wins the knight, as 38...♖b2+ and 39...♖a1+ mating is threatened.

31...♘e4! 32 ♖c4

32 fxe3 ♘xd2 33 ♖c2 ♘xf3+ leaves Black a piece ahead.

32...♘xf2! 33 ♗g2 ♗e6 34 ♖cc2 ♘g4+ 35 ♔h3

35 ♔h1 ♖a1+.

35...♘e5+ 36 ♔h2 ♖xf3 37 ♖xe2 ♘g4+ 38 ♔h3 ♘e3+ 39 ♔h2 ♘xc2 40 ♗xf3 ♘d4!

The 'sting in the tail', which Alekhine made his trademark.

41 ♖f2 ♘xf3+ 42 ♖xf3 ♗d5 0-1

Aron Nimzowitsch (1886-1935)

Nimzowitsch was the first of the Hypermoderns, and one of the most imaginative players of all time. He was a highly-strung character, who reputedly practised yoga and even headstands between moves and maintained a bitter feud with his ideological opposite Tarrasch. Nimzowitsch regarded himself as the crown prince of chess, but failed to raise the stake money after Capablanca had accepted his challenge in 1926, or to find backers for a later match with Alekhine.

Nimzowitsch's manifesto, *My System*, was published in 1925 and remains essential reading to this day. He was the first to challenge the classical conception of the centre, and showed that a cramped position need not be bad if it could support a freeing move. The other pillar of his system was his theory of blockade, which advocated the over-protection of one's own strong points and restraint of the opponent's active possibilities.

Johner-Nimzowitsch
Dresden 1926
1 d4 ♘f6 2 c4 e6 3 ♘c3 ♗b4

This is the starting position of the Nimzo-Indian Defence, the greatest of Nimzowitsch's many contributions to opening theory. Criticised by Tarrasch for playing 'ugly' moves, Nimzo retorted that true beauty lies in the thought behind a move, not its outward appearance. The idea here is to fight for control of e4 without committing himself to an early ...d5.

4 e3 0-0 5 ♗d3 c5 6 ♘f3 ♘c6 7 0-0 ♗xc3

This is the second point: Black gladly concedes the two bishops, intending to blockade the position and lay siege to the doubled c-pawns.

8 bxc3 d6 9 ♘d2 b6 10 ♘b3

This is a useful manoeuvre, anticipating Black's plan of ...♗a6, ...♘a5 and ...♖c8 with strong pressure on c4.

10...e5 11 f4 e4 12 ♗e2 ♕d7

White was hoping for g4-g5 with attacking chances, but Nimzowitsch finds a startling plan to restrain this possibility.

13 h3 ♘e7 14 ♕e1 h5! 15 ♗d2

15 ♕h4 ♘f5 16 ♕g5 ♘h7 17 ♕xh5 ♘g3 wins the exchange.

15...♕f5 16 ♔h2 ♕h7!

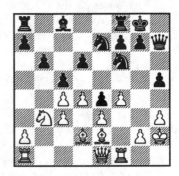

An amazing idea! But now it is White's king that looks more vulnerable.

17 a4 ♘f5 18 g3 a5

Of course Black maintains his queenside blockade.

19 ♖g1 ♘h6 20 ♗f1 ♗d7 21 ♗c1 ♖ac8 22 d5

White loses patience, clarifying the central position, but in any case he had few prospects of activating his bishops.

22...♔h8 23 ♘d2 ♖g8 24 ♗g2 g5 25 ♘f1 ♖g7 26 ♖a2 ♘f5 27 ♗h1 ♖cg8 28 ♕d1 gxf4 29 exf4 ♗c8

An instructive moment: before launching his kingside attack, Nimzowitsch repositions his bishop on a more active square.

30 ♕b3 ♗a6

31 ♖e2

31 ♗d2 ♖g6 32 ♗e1 ♘g4+! 33 hxg4 hxg4+ 34 ♔g2 ♗xc4 35 ♕xc4 e3! 36 ♘xe3 (otherwise 36...♕h3#) 36...♘xe3+ picks up the queen.

31...♘h4! 32 ♖e3

32 ♘d2 is met by 32...♗c8! – now that the white queen has been lured to the queenside, the bishop switches back to menace the kingside, e.g. 33 ♕d1 ♗xh3! 34 ♔xh3 ♕f5+ 35 ♔h2 ♘g4+ 36 ♔h3 ♘f2+ 37 ♔h2 ♕h3# or 33 ♘xe4 33...♕f5 34 ♘f2 ♕xh3+!! 35 ♘xh3 ♘g4#.

32...♗c8! 33 ♕c2 ♗xh3!

Once again, the bishop sacrifices itself to strip away the king's defences.

34 ♗xe4

34 ♔xh3 ♕f5+ 35 ♔h2 ♘g4+ 36 ♔h3 ♘f2+ 37 ♔xh4 ♕h3#.

34...♗f5 35 ♗xf5 ♘xf5 36 ♖e2 h4 37 ♖gg2 hxg3+ 38 ♔g1 ♕h3 39 ♘e3 ♘h4 40 ♔f1 ♖e8!

There is no need to take the exchange at once – it isn't going anywhere.

0-1

Since 41 ♔e1 ♘f3+ and 42...♕h1+ mates, and White has no defence to 41...♘xg2 42 ♖xg2 (42 ♘xg2 ♕h1#) 42...♕h1+ 43 ♖g1 (43 ♔e2 ♕xg2+ and the knight is pinned) 43...♕f3+ 44 ♔e1 ♖xe3+ 45 ♗xe3 ♕xe3+ with an extra piece.

Richard Réti (1889-1929)

Although Réti represented Czechoslovakia after the war, he was born in Hungary, and began his chess career in Vienna, where he went to study mathematics and physics. He played his first master tournament there in 1908, scoring a catastrophic 1½ out of 19 and finishing last. Réti worked closely with Gyula Breyer, a gifted player who died very young, developing a radical new approach to the game. Réti emerged as a top player, winning major tournaments from 1918 onwards, but lacked the competitive streak necessary to challenge for the supreme title. He was a genial, absent-minded intellectual, motivated by beauty and strategic depth rather than practical results.

Réti was the spokesman for his generation, chronicling the development of chess strategy in two classic books, *Modern Ideas in Chess* and

Masters of the Chessboard. In contrast to the scattergun genius of Nimzowitsch, Réti gave the chess world an accessible and balanced exposition of the Hypermodern theories in both theory and practice.

Max Euwe (1901-1981)

Euwe became Dutch champion aged 20, but refused to be diverted from his career as a mathematician. After completing his doctorate in 1926, he stepped up his chess activities. A series of impressive tournament results, combined with narrow defeats in matches against Alekhine, Bogoljubow and Capablanca, established Euwe as a worthy challenger for the world title. However, his professional commitments prevented him from building on his unexpected success, and he lost the rematch heavily.

After Alekhine's death in possession of the title, FIDE met in 1947 to decide how to choose his successor. Euwe, as the previous holder, was declared champion pending the contest for the title; the next day, the USSR delegation arrived and had the decision annulled! The World Championship match-tournament was held in 1948, split between The Hague and Moscow. Euwe finished last by a huge margin, signalling the end of his world title aspirations; however, he continued to popularise chess in his own country, winning the national championship thirteen times. He returned to the world stage as President of FIDE from 1970 to 1978, an unenviable task as Fischer first took the World Championship at Reykjavik in 1972 amid huge controversy and then abdicated by making demands that FIDE, dominated by a Soviet bloc and Third World majority, would not agree to.

Euwe's chess style was logical and correct rather than innovative; he was well prepared in the opening and calculated variations accurately.

Mikhail Botvinnik (1911-1995)

Botvinnik learned chess at 12, quite late by today's standards, but progressed to the master title within four years by virtue of the discipline and hard work that became his trademark. His studies in electrical engineering did not unduly detain him, and in 1931 he became USSR Champion. He also took the Championship in 1933, 1939, 1941, 1944, 1945 and 1952.

By this time, the Communists were showing great interest in chess, not least because Lenin and Trotsky both played, but also as a means of educating the people. Above all, they coveted the intellectual high ground that a Soviet World Champion would bring, and it was Botvinnik who was chosen to carry out this mission.

After an initial disappointment at Hastings 1934/5, he responded with an excellent result in 1936, tying with Capablanca at the Nottingham International Tournament in which three other world champions played. and winning the AVRO tournament at Amsterdam in 1938.

He was a confirmed communist; after his victory at Nottingham he sent a now famous letter to Stalin that began: "Dear beloved leader and teacher ... this was only possible because I sensed behind me ... that daily care which you, our great leader has taken ... to rear in us representatives of Soviet youth a healthy and joyful generation in all fields of our socialist reconstruction".

He was a Party favourite, even being excused wartime duties to continue his work on chess; it paid off at the World Championship match-tournament of 1948. The final scores were: Botvinnik 14/20; Smyslov 11; Keres, Reshevsky 10½; Euwe 4.

Botvinnik was no less proficient off the board: when FIDE drew up the new rules of engagement, he secured the right to retain his title in the event of a drawn match, and to a rematch the following year if he lost. He took full advantage of these privileges, winning only two matches out of seven, but holding the title for 13 of the next 15 years! The rematch clause no longer applied in 1963, and Botvinnik bowed out of the championship cycle after losing to Petrosian.

Unusually, he rarely drunk and smoked only briefly. "I got drunk on vodka after winning the Soviet Championship in 1931 and never did it again."

After retiring from play in 1970, Botvinnik set up his famous chess school, whose alumni include Karpov and Kasparov, and worked on a computer program to reproduce the thought processes of a human master, albeit with rather less success.

Botvinnik-Capablanca
Amsterdam AVRO 1938

1 d4 ♘f6 2 c4 e6 3 ♘c3 ♗b4 4 e3 d5 5 a3 ♗xc3+ 6 bxc3 c5 7 cxd5 exd5

The early ...d5 has allowed White to acquire the bishop pair and undouble his troublesome c-pawns. This line became known as Botvinnik's Variation after the Soviet champion's famous victory here.

8 ♗d3 0-0 9 ♘e2

The natural 9 ♘f3 is a mistake, as White's plan is to construct a broad pawn centre with f3 and e4.

9...b6 10 0-0 ♗a6 11 ♗xa6

Perhaps even stronger is 11 f3 ♗xd3 12 ♕xd3 ♖e8 13 ♘g3 intending ♖a2-e2.

11...♘xa6 12 ♗b2 ♕d7 13 a4 ♖fe8 14 ♕d3 c4?

This is a rare positional error from Capablanca, who clearly under-estimated the danger facing him on the kingside. Although the a4-pawn can hardly be saved in the long run, the release of tension on d4 allows White's central phalanx to start rolling unopposed.

15 ♕c2 ♘b8 16 ♖ae1 ♘c6 17 ♘g3 ♘a5 18 f3 ♘b3 19 e4 ♕xa4 20 e5 ♘d7 21 ♕f2 g6 22 f4 f5

This allows White to open lines against the king, but otherwise f5-f6, ♕f4-h6 and ♖f4-h4 with mating threats on g7 and h7 was hard to meet — while his dark squares collapse, Black's queen is stranded on a4 after its pawn-grabbing expedition.

23 exf6 ♘xf6 24 f5 ♖xe1 25 ♖xe1 ♖e8 26 ♖e6 ♖xe6 27 fxe6

The passed pawn on e6 is a dangerous attacking unit in its own right, let alone a potential queen.

27...♔g7 28 ♕f4 ♕e8 29 ♕e5 ♕e7

30 ♗a3!!

The bad bishop wakes up, making a stunning sacrifice to decoy the black queen.

30...♕xa3 31 ♘h5+! gxh5 32 ♕g5+ ♔f8 33 ♕xf6+ ♔g8 34 e7

Black's checks soon run out, and his far-flung pieces can do nothing to stop the e-pawn queening.

34...♕c1+ 35 ♔f2 ♕c2+ 36 ♔g3 ♕d3+ 37 ♔h4 ♕e4+ 38 ♔xh5 ♕e2+ 39 ♔h4 ♕e4+ 40 g4 ♕e1+ 41 ♔h5 1-0

Vasily Smyslov (1921-)

Taught by his father, himself an expert, from the age of six, Smyslov learned quickly: he shared first place in the Moscow Championship aged 17, and became a USSR Grandmaster three years later. He was musically gifted as well, almost making

the grade as a baritone with the Bolshoi Opera. However, after his second place in the 1948 World Championship tournament, he struggled to keep pace with the likes of Bronstein, Keres and Geller.

Smyslov's form returned in the Candidates tournament of Zurich 1953, where he scored 18/28 to finish two points clear of the field. But after drawing a title match with Botvinnik in a fluctuating struggle, Smyslov had to qualify all over again. He won the next Candidates, Amsterdam 1956, and finished the job convincingly the following year, but his brief reign was ended in the 1958 rematch. Smyslov stayed at the top, remarkably reaching the Candidates' Final aged 63, before bowing out to a youthful Kasparov. Even today he remains a top class player, regularly humbling youthful adversaries and is surpassed in this regard only by Viktor Korchnoi.

Mikhail Tal (1936-1992)

The young Tal terrorised the chess establishment in the 1950s with a sacrificial attacking style in stark contrast to the rational positional play of Smyslov and Botvinnik. He set new records as the youngest USSR Champion (20) and World Champion (23), but lost the rematch to Botvinnik after poor health had disrupted his preparations. He was a hard drinker and a heavy smoker, even a morphine addict in the late 1960s. Tal would also be awarded the title of World Hangover Champion had it ever been awarded. In one celebrated case he stayed up all night at a World Cup tournament in Reykjavik playing blitz, drinking and smoking despite having been admitted to hospital and discharging himself. The next morning Tal had to play Black against Kasparov but he made an easy draw! I recall a simultaneous display he gave in Liverpool when I was a child. Prior to travelling to the event he downed five double whiskies in quick succession while crushing the top players of the host club at blitz and then declared he was ready to go. The simul was amazing. Tal ripped through the opposition with queen sacrifices and combinations of all kinds. He had these piercing eyes and a birth defect which had left him with just three fingers one hand. I will never forget the sight of one poor hapless opponent who was totally movebound after about an hour – the fear in his eyes as Tal approached!

Tal suffered recurring kidney trouble throughout his life however, the 'magician from Riga' cared little for his health, let alone titles, money or possessions: all that mattered was his next beautiful combination. Here is one.

Tal-Hecht
Varna OL 1962

1 d4 ♘f6 2 c4 e6 3 ♘f3 b6 4 ♘c3 ♗b4 5 ♗g5 ♗b7 6 e3 h6 7 ♗h4 ♗xc3+ 8 bxc3 d6 9 ♘d2 e5

Once again in the Nimzo-Indian, Black willingly concedes the two bishops to double the white c-pawns,

and sets about blockading the dark squares.

10 f3 ♕e7 11 e4 ♘bd7 12 ♗d3 ♘f8 13 c5!?

A typically aggressive solution from Tal, opening the position for his bishops for the price of a pawn – and a doubled one at that.

13...dxc5

13...bxc5 14 d5 with good play on the queenside.

14 dxe5 ♕xe5 15 ♕a4+ c6?!

This is inaccurate, as it weakens the important d6-square; after 15...♘6d7 16 ♕c2 White's compensation would have been sufficient, but no more.

16 0-0

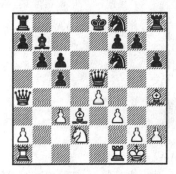

16...♘g6

16...♕xc3 17 ♗a6 (17 ♘c4 b5 18 ♘d6+ ♔d7 19 ♘xb5 cxb5 20 ♗xb5+ also gives compensation, e.g. 20...♔e7 21 e5 ♕d4+ 22 ♕xd4 cxd4 23 exf6+ gxf6 24 ♖fe1+ ♘e6 25 ♖ad1 with the idea of f4-f5) 17...♗xa6 18 ♕xc6+ ♔e7 19 e5 ♕d4+ (19...♖d8 20 exf6+ gxf6 21 ♖fe1+ ♘e6 22 ♘e4 ♕d4+ 23 ♔h1 and f6 caves in) 20 ♗f2 ♕d8 21 exf6+ gxf6 22 ♘e4 ♘e6 23 ♖fd1

♕c7 24 ♗xc5+ bxc5 25 ♕xa6 with continuing pressure against Black's scattered pawns and exposed king.

17 ♘c4 ♕e6

17...b5 18 ♘xe5 bxa4 19 ♘xg6 fxg6 20 e5 is dreadful for Black.

18 e5!

Tal is obliged to make heavy sacrifices to keep the black king in the centre.

18...b5

18...♘xh4 19 ♘d6+ ♔f8 and now, rather than take any of the three (!) pieces on offer, Tal intended to build up further with 20 ♖ae1!.

19 exf6!?

At this point in the game, the Argentine GM Miguel Najdorf came up and kissed Tal!

19...bxa4?

19...0-0! 20 ♖ae1 ♕xe1! (20...♕d5 21 ♕c2 ♘xh4 22 ♘e5 with an attack) 21 ♖xe1 bxa4 is best, when Tal's suggested 22 ♗xg6 fxg6 23 ♖e7 is met by 23...g5! (23...♖f7? 24 ♘d6) 24 ♖xg7+ ♔h8 25 ♗g3 ♗a6, when White is running out of compensation.

20 fxg7 ♖g8 21 ♗f5!!

21...♘xh4

21...♕xc4 leaves Black a whole queen ahead, but still unable to resist the attack on his king: 22 ♖fe1+ ♕e6 23 ♖xe6+ fxe6 24 ♗xg6+ ♔d7 25 ♖d1+ ♔c7 26 ♗g3+ ♔b6 27 ♖b1+ ♔a6 28 ♗d3+ ♔a5 29 ♗c7#.

21...♕xf5 22 ♘d6+ ♔d7 23 ♘xf5 ♘xh4 24 ♘xh4 promises good play against Black's shattered pawns.

22 ♗xe6 ♗a6

22...fxe6 23 ♘d6+ and 24 ♘xb7 is no use, but how is Tal to save his piece now?

23 ♘d6+ ♔e7 24 ♗c4! ♖xg7 25 g3 ♔xd6?!

Black should have exchanged his opponent's bishop, as now he has the worse minor piece to add to his problems.

26 ♗xa6 ♘f5 27 ♖ab1 f6 28 ♖fd1+ ♔e7 29 ♖e1+ ♔d6 30 ♔f2 c4

This is rather panicky; Black should have supported his knight with 30...h5.

31 g4 ♘e7 32 ♖b7 ♖ag8 33 ♗xc4 ♘d5 34 ♗xd5 cxd5 35 ♖b4 ♖c8

Probably drained by the earlier play, Black misses the chance to exchange off some of his weak pawns with 35...h5 36 h3 hxg4 37 hxg4 f5.

36 ♖xa4 ♖xc3 37 ♖a6+ ♔c5 38 ♖xf6 h5 39 h3 hxg4 40 hxg4

The emergence of connected passed pawns spells defeat for Black.

40...♖h7 41 g5 ♖h5 42 ♖f5 ♖c2+ 43 ♔g3 ♔c4 44 ♖ee5 d4 45 g6 ♖h1 46 ♖c5+ ♔d3 47 ♖xc2 ♔xc2 48 ♔f4 ♖g1 49 ♖g5 1-0

Tigran Petrosian (1929-1984)

Petrosian was born to working-class Armenian parents in Tbilisi, Georgia. After his parents died when he was 16, Petrosian took over his father's job as a caretaker, but soon decided to return to his roots in Armenia. He won the republic's championship twice, and moved to Moscow in 1949 to meet the strongest opposition. Petrosian first qualified for the Candidates tournament in 1953, but only at the fourth attempt, in Curaçao 1962, did he qualify for a world title challenge.

This tournament proved highly controversial, with Korchnoi and Fischer complaining bitterly of collusion between Petrosian, Keres and Geller. These three drew all of their games against each other without a fight − in a quadruple-round all-play-all − saving their energy for the five other competitors. Keres was arguably the biggest loser on the deal. In the final cycle, he adjourned with a slight disadvantage against Benko, a player he had always beaten in the past. Putting all ethical and political considerations to one side, Petrosian's wife mobilised the Soviet contingent to analyse the position with Benko; the US repre-

sentative won the game, and Keres finished second by just half a point. The Candidates cycle has taken the form of knockout matches ever since.

The wily Armenian duly overcame the ageing Botvinnik, and succeeded in his first title defence against Spassky. Even after his defeat in 1969, Petrosian qualified for every Candidates cycle until 1980. Despite his outstanding results, Petrosian was accused of playing too defensively and never won more than grudging admiration from the chess public. His apparently bizarre manoeuvres, inspired by Nimzowitsch's theory of prophylaxis, were simply too far ahead of their time to be properly appreciated. In my opinion he was misunderstood and when roused he could play great attacking chess and marvellous sacrifices.

Dückstein-Petrosian
Varna OL 1962

1 e4 c6 2 d4 d5 3 ♘c3 dxe4 4 ♘xe4 ♗f5 5 ♘g3 ♗g6 6 ♘f3 ♘d7 7 ♗d3

It is normal in this variation for White to gain space on the kingside with 7 h4 h6 8 h5 ♗h7 before offering this exchange. However, the downside of this operation is that the h5-pawn may become weak in the endgame.

7...e6 8 0-0 ♕c7 9 c4 0-0-0 10 ♗xg6

The disadvantage of not chasing the bishop to h7 is revealed: Black is no longer obliged to play ...♗xd3, but waits for White to initiate the exchange of bishops. This allows him to open a file against the enemy king.

10...hxg6 11 ♕a4 ♔b8 12 b4

White begins a pawn storm, but the black position is very solid.

12...♘h6 13 ♕b3 ♘f5 14 a4 e5!

Opening the centre – the classic response to an attack on the wing.

15 dxe5 ♘xe5 16 ♘xe5 ♕xe5 17 ♗b2 ♕c7 18 c5 a5!!

A completely unexpected defensive move: usually it is a mistake to weaken the pawns defending the king, but in this case Petrosian sees that it is more important to undermine the pawn on c5.

19 ♖ad1 ♖xd1 20 ♖xd1 ♖h4

The rook takes full advantage of its half-open file to reach a superb position.

21 bxa5 ♗xc5 22 a6 b6 23 ♖e1 ♔a7 24 ♗e5 ♕d7 25 ♘e4 ♗d4 26 g3 *(See next diagram)* **26...♗xe5!**

Petrosian sacrifices the exchange, but takes total control of the position. His own king is perfectly safe, in marked contrast to its opposite number.

27 gxh4 ♘d4 28 ♕d1 ♕d5 29 ♖e3 ♘f5 30 ♖e1 ♘d4

Petrosian repeats moves to gain time on the clock, and to show his opponent who's boss.

31 ♕d3 f5 32 ♘g5 c5 33 ♖e3 c4 34 ♕d1

Returning the exchange with 34 ♖xe5 ♕xe5 35 ♕xc4 might have offered more hope of counterplay, although Black's queen and knight remain menacingly placed.

34...♗xa6 35 ♖a3

35 ♘f3 (35 ♘e6 f4 36 ♘xd4 fxe3 37 fxe3 ♕e4 also sees Black well on top) 35...♘xf3+ 36 ♕xf3 ♕xf3 37 ♖xf3 c3 and the c-pawn will cost White his rook.

35...♗f6 36 h3 f4 37 ♕g4

37 ♘f3 ♘xf3+ 38 ♕xf3 ♕xf3 39 ♖xf3 ♗e5 is similar to the previous note.

37...♔a5!!

Now that White's pieces have lost all co-ordination, Petrosian brings his king into play to support the c-pawn.

38 ♘f3

38 ♕d1 ♔b4 39 ♖a2 c3.

38...♔b4 39 ♘xd4 ♔xa3 40 ♘c2+ ♔xa4 0-1

41 ♕xf4 ♕d1+ picks up the knight, so White is two pawns down with a lost position.

Boris Spassky (1937-)

Spassky was a popular world champion, unusually modest for someone so talented, but he suffered from a lack of self-confidence. He became world junior champion with ease in 1955, but was overtaken by Tal as he repeatedly failed his most critical tests. In 1961, Spassky divorced his first wife – 'We were like bishops of opposite colour' was his verdict – and changed his trainer. He replaced Tolush, a brilliant attacking player but something of a bully, with Bondarevsky, whose friendship and expertise relaunched Spassky's career. After losing to Petrosian, Spassky predicted that he would be back, and so it turned out. He was regarded as the complete player, and a worthy champion.

However, Spassky became yet another victim of the post-title blues. He made no secret of his natural laziness, played few tournaments and scored indifferent results. He appeared to lack the will-power to resist Fischer's intense onslaught, and suffered a crushing defeat. The loss of the world title, to an American at that, was seen as a national disaster ("It was like something was wrong with our culture" – Bronstein) and Spassky's future looked bleak. He mustered all his strength to win the 1973 USSR Championship, but lost his Candidates semi-final to the new favourite, Karpov. In 1975, and not a moment too soon, Spassky was allowed to settle in Paris after marrying a French diplomat. He rarely shows his attacking skills nowadays,

preferring a relaxing game of tennis to the stress of fighting chess – and who can blame him.

Larsen-Spassky
USSR-RoW, Belgrade 1970
1 b3
This unusual opening is called the Nimzowitsch-Larsen Attack after its two most eminent advocates. The Danish GM was deeply influenced by Nimzowitsch, who spent his later years in Copenhagen.
1...e5 2 ♗b2 ♘c6 3 c4 ♘f6 4 ♘f3?!
This is too provocative; when the players met again, a few weeks later, Larsen went for a 'hedgehog' formation with 4 e3 d5 5 cxd5 ♘xd5 6 a3.
4...e4 5 ♘d4 ♗c5 6 ♘xc6 dxc6
Breaking the general rule which is capture towards the centre but clearly better than 6...bxc6, as it releases the bishop and opens the d-file for the queen. The e4-pawn cramps White's position, but will become a liability if it is not properly supported.
7 e3 ♗f5 8 ♕c2 ♕e7 9 ♗e2 0-0-0 10 f4?
This is a reckless weakening of the e1-h4 diagonal, which White soon regrets. Larsen must have under-estimated Spassky's reply, as otherwise he would have acquiesced to a slight disadvantage with, say, 10 ♘f3.
10...♘g4! 11 g3
11 ♗xg4 ♕h4+ 12 g3 ♕xg4 does not even bear thinking about, as it would leave White defenceless on the light squares.

11...h5! 12 h3

12 ♗xg7 ♖hg8 is very risky for White, as it opens lines with his king stranded in the centre.

12...h4!

13 hxg4

13 ♗xg4 ♗xg4 14 hxg4 hxg3 15 ♖g1 is met by 15...♖h1!! 16 ♖xh1 g2 17 ♖g1 ♕h4+ 18 ♔e2 (18 ♔d1 ♕f2) 18...♕xg4+ 19 ♔e1 ♕g3+ 20 ♔e2 ♗xe3! and Black either mates or gains a second queen.

13...hxg3 14 ♖g1 ♖h1!!

15 ♖xh1

15 ♔f1 ♖xg1+ 16 ♔xg1 ♕h4 mates quickly.

15...g2 16 ♖f1

16 ♖g1 ♕h4+ 17 ♔d1 ♕h1 wins easily.

16...♕h4+ 17 ♔d1 gxf1♕+ 0-1

Mate is forced after 18 ♗xf1 ♗xg4+ 19 ♔c1 (19 ♗e2 ♕h1#) 19...♕e1+.

Bobby Fischer (1943-)

Bobby Fischer is the one man who can turn chess into headline news. Totally consumed by the game from the age of six, he saw no reason to fit in at his Brooklyn high school, although he is said to have swapped *MAD* comics with classmate Barbra Streisand. Fischer was US champion at 14 and a Candidate at 15, leaving school to turn professional the following year. The events of Curacao 1962 strengthened his belief that there was a Soviet conspiracy to prevent him winning the title. Fischer withdrew from international competition for three years in protest, missing the next championship cycle but scoring an unparalleled 11/11 in the 1963/4 US championship.

Fischer again ruined his chances in the 1967 Sousse interzonal. After a strong start, he withdrew from the tournament over a trivial dispute concerning his playing schedule. Fischer's next chance was the 1970 US championship, which doubled as a qualifying tournament for the interzonal. Yet again, he forfeited his challenge, refusing to participate as he considered the playing conditions unsatisfactory. It is only fair to point out that Fischer's uncompromising stance on improved pay and conditions for professional chess players was well-motivated and generally successful, but he paid heavily for his refusal to make the slightest concession.

Fischer was granted a reprieve, when his compatriot Benko generously gave up his place in the interzonal. Fischer destroyed the opposition, scoring 18½/23 to finish 3½ points clear of Larsen in second. In the Candidates matches, he whitewashed first Taimanov and then Larsen 6-0, before crushing Petrosian 6½-2½ – results which remain unmatched to this day. The match with Spassky, at the height of the Cold War, captured the imagination of the world. Could the unruly American single-handedly destroy the Soviet monopoly? Would he even turn up?

The scheduled date for the first game in Reykjavik came and went, with Fischer still in New York haggling over conditions. The English financier Jim Slater added £50,000 from his own pocket to the official purse of $125,000, telling Fischer 'If you aren't afraid of Spassky then I have removed the element of money'. Fischer did not appreciate the insinuation of cowardice on his part, and promptly flew to Iceland. He went 2-0 behind, losing the first game with a totally unnecessary piece sacrifice in a level position, and defaulting the second in protest at the presence of television cameras in the playing area. His insistence that the organisers check the light fittings for KGB electronic devices led to the discovery of two dead flies. After this, however, it was one-way traffic and Fischer finally achieved his life's ambition.

Fischer was the complete player and the first champion to play a truly broad repertoire; he opened with both 1 e4, and 1 c4 against Spassky and played a variety of defences with Black. His most famous contribution to opening theory was the Poisoned Pawn variation of the Sicilian Najdorf, which nowadays is championed by Kasparov.

Fischer then withdrew completely from chess and nobody really knows why. In 1974, Karpov earned the right to challenge him, but it was not to be. Fischer demanded an openended match, the winner being the first player to win ten games. He also insisted on retaining his title if the score reached 9-9, effectively forcing Karpov to win by two clear games. FIDE, dominated by the KGB-controlled USSR Chess Federation rejected the second proposal and Fischer duly resigned the FIDE title – although he considers himself the undefeated world champion to this day.

Fischer again stunned the chess world in 1992, when he returned from his self-imposed exile to play another match with Spassky. This took place in Serbia, in defiance of UN sanctions, with a $5 million prize fund contributed by one Jezdimir Vasiljevic, whose fortune had been made in mysterious circumstances. Fischer tantalised everyone who wondered just how good he could be after such a prolonged absence by winning the first game in superb style, but after that the quality of play declined somewhat.

Fischer won 10-5 (the fifteen draws not counting) but the result was incidental as Fischer used the match as a platform to air his increasingly irrational and unsavoury grievances against the rest of the world.

Fischer-Benko

Belgrade/Bled/Zagreb Ct 1959

1 e4 c5 2 ♘f3 ♘c6 3 d4 cxd4 4 ♘xd4 ♘f6 5 ♘c3 d6 6 ♗c4

This bishop move became Fischer's antidote to the Sicilian Defence and he scored many fine wins with it.

6...♕b6 7 ♘de2 e6 8 0-0 ♗e7 9 ♗b3 0-0 10 ♔h1 ♘a5

It is advisable to exchange the Bishop on b3 before White plays f4-f5 attacking e6.

11 ♗g5 ♕c5 12 f4 b5 13 ♘g3 b4 Fischer's *My 60 Memorable Games* (Batsford) mentions a comment by Gligoric who gives 13...♗b7; Fischer recommends 13...♘xb3.

14 e5 dxe5

14...♘xb3 15 exf6 gxf6 16 ♗h6 Threatens ♕g4+ mating so White wins; 14...bxc3 15 exf6 ♗xf6 16 ♗xf6 gxf6 17 ♘e4 ♕f5 18 ♘xd6 ♕g6 19 ♖f3 with a decisive attack – Udovcic.

15 ♗xf6 gxf6

15...♗xf6 16 ♘ce4 ♕e7 17 ♘h5! ♔h8 18 ♘exf6 gxf6 19 fxe5 fxe5 20 ♘f6 followed by ♕h5.

15...bxc3! 16 ♘e4 ♕b4 17 ♕g4 ♗xf6 18 ♘xf6+ ♔h8 19 ♕h4 h6 (19...gxf6 20 ♕xf6+ ♔g8 21 ♖f3) 20 ♘g4 threatening 21 ♘xh6 and if 20...♔h7, 21 fxe5 threatens ♘f6+ winning the queen.

16 ♘ce4 ♕d4 17 ♕h5

White is attacking with queen, two knights and a rook with another rook on the way. It's not surprising that Black is defenceless.

17...♘xb3 18 ♕h6 exf4

18...♘xa1 19 ♘h5.

19 ♘h5 f5 20 ♖ad1 ♕e5 21 ♘ef6+ ♗xf6 22 ♘xf6+ ♕xf6 23 ♕xf6

"Now it's skin and bones" – Fischer.

23...♘c5 24 ♕g5+ ♔h8 25 ♕e7 ♗a6 26 ♕xc5 ♗xf1 27 ♖xf1 1-0

Viktor Korchnoi (1931-)

Korchnoi spent the war years in Leningrad, suffering great hardship in the siege of 1941-3; this experience undoubtedly developed the superhuman fighting spirit and tenacity that have characterised his chess career. Korchnoi took on the system single-handed rather than play by the Communists' rules, but faced ever greater obstacles as the black marks accumulated in his KGB file. After giving an outspoken interview at Amsterdam 1976, Korchnoi realised that he dare not return home, and was granted asylum in Holland.

Korchnoi's defection caused the Soviets great embarrassment, all the more so as he eliminated Petrosian, Polugaevsky and Spassky from the Candidates cycle. Unable to mention the name of a 'non-person', the Soviet press would say that their man had lost, but not to whom! The table for the Korchnoi-Spassky in 1978 had a board underneath to stop the players kicking each other; Spassky preferred to consider the position from a rest area, only coming to the board to execute his move.

This was but a warm-up for the Battle of Baguio City. Korchnoi protested that he could not play on equal terms while his wife and son remained in the USSR. He objected to Baturinsky, a former KGB prosecutor, leading Karpov's delegation. He threatened to beat up the 'parapsychologist' Dr Zukhar, whose function appeared to be to sit in the audience and stare at him. Korchnoi played with reflective glasses to counter this. Even his pet owl died of a mystery illness early in the match.

Korchnoi's camp rose to the occasion when Karpov's team brought him a yoghurt during the second game, mischievously suggesting that the choice of refreshment might represent a coded message. Eventually it was agreed that Karpov could be served a blueberry yoghurt at 7.15 p.m. Korchnoi's play suffered as the backstage antics fuelled his paranoia, but he fought back heroically after befriending two members of the highly dubious Ananda Marga cult. Fortified by a combination of medi-

tation and headstands, Korchnoi retrieved a three game deficit, only to fall at the final hurdle. Although he did not lose the match intentionally, Korchnoi feared for his life if he won; years later, Tal told him that the KGB were ready to arrange an 'accident' if need be.

Korchnoi remains a ferocious competitor to this day; aged 64, he claimed first place at Madrid 1995 ahead of top class opposition. Consistently a queen's pawn player, Korchnoi was the scourge of the King's Indian Defence and an inveterate pawn grabber.

Anatoly Karpov (1951-)

In the aftermath of the Reykjavik debacle, Karpov was chosen as the new Soviet hero. None of the previous champions matched the Communist ideal – Botvinnik, Smyslov and Spassky all had Jewish connections, Petrosian was Armenian and Tal a Jew from Latvia – but Karpov, the 1969 world junior champion, was an all-Russian, working-class lad. Karpov received massive State support for his Candidates matches, and overcame Polugaevsky, Spassky and Korchnoi in turn. However, the Soviet authorities had no intention of risking him in a match with Fischer in 1975: recently released KGB documents reveal that they had planned to frustrate negotiations with demands unacceptable to the American.

Karpov himself wanted to play the match, rather than win a cheapened title by default. He soon proved himself a worthy champion, winning almost every top level tournament for a decade. His 1978 match with the defector Korchnoi was bitterly contested in every sense; Karpov finally achieved the decisive sixth win after letting a 5-2 lead slip to 5-5. The KGB kept Korchnoi's wife and son as hostage in the USSR throughout his battles with Karpov. Karpov's third match with Korchnoi was comparatively routine, but his first with Kasparov was truly extraordinary. 4-0 ahead after only 9 games, Karpov apparently decided to avoid taking any risks himself and wait for Kasparov to make mistakes and lose two more games and the match. A series of seventeen, generally short and boring, draws ensued before Karpov won again. In Game 31, he missed a chance to complete a humiliating whitewash, and the tide began to turn. Karpov lost game 32, his first ever defeat against Kasparov, plodded through fourteen more draws, lost games 47 and 48 horribly, and then ... the match was called off!

FIDE president Campomanes claimed that the stress of the five-month match was endangering the health of the players. Despite still being one match from defeat Kasparov was furious and thus started a long running feud. Campomanes, whose electoral success rested on the votes of the Soviet bloc, no doubt felt obliged to protect Karpov; he had considered a similar intervention in 1978, when Korchnoi started fighting back.

Despite pushing Kasparov to the limit in their four subsequent matches, Karpov could not wrest the title from his 'perpetual opponent' at the board. However, it fell into his lap in 1993, when FIDE called upon him to contest the 'official' world championship against Timman – whose record against Karpov is dire – after Kasparov decided to make his own arrangements to play Short. Having won a tarnished crown for the second time, Karpov silenced his critics with an astonishing score of 11/13 at Linares 1994 – probably the greatest result in the greatest tournament of all time.

Karpov-Kamsky
Moscow 1992
1 d4 ♘f6 2 c4 g6 3 ♘f3 ♗g7 4 g3 c6 5 ♗g2 d5 6 cxd5 cxd5 7 ♘c3 0-0 8 ♘e5 e6 9 0-0

The position is almost symmetrical, but the advantage of moving first has enabled White to plant a knight on e5.

9...♘fd7 10 f4

10...♘c6

10...♘xe5 (10...f6 11 ♘d3 with an edge for White) 11 fxe5 ♘c6 12 e4! (this opens the position to get at the weak dark squares) 12...dxe4 13 ♗e3 f5 14 exf6 ♖xf6 15 ♘xe4 ♖xf1+ 16 ♕xf1 brought White a quick win in Kasparov-Nunn, Brussels 1986: 16...♘xd4? 17 ♖d1 e5 18 ♘g5 1-0. Play could have continued 18...♕e7 19 ♗d5+ ♗e6 20 ♖xd4 exd4 21 ♗xe6+ ♔h8 22 ♘f7+ ♔g8 23 ♘d8+ ♔h8 24 ♗g5! ♕b4 25 ♘f7+ ♔g8 26 ♘e5+ ♔h8 27 ♘xg6+ hxg6 28 ♕h3+.

11 ♗e3 ♘b6 12 ♗f2 ♗d7 13 e4 ♘e7 14 ♘xd7 ♕xd7 15 e5 ♖ac8

The contours of the position are set: White will play for a kingside attack with f5, while Black seeks counterplay on the open c-file.

16 ♖c1 a6 17 b3!?

A double-edged move: the knight on b6 is deprived of the c4-outpost, but the dark squares on the queenside are weakened.

17...♖c7 18 ♕d2 ♖fc8 19 g4 ♗f8 20 ♕e3!

'Creeping' queen moves are a Karpov speciality; here, the point is to set up a skewer with ♗h3, as detailed in the next note.

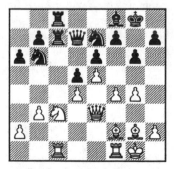

20...♘c6 21 f5 ♗a3

21...exf5 22 gxf5 ♕xf5 23 ♗h3! (23 ♘e2 is also possible, sacrificing

the pawn for a dangerous initiative, but perhaps not in Karpov's style) 23...♕h5 24 ♗xc8 ♗h6 (anything Karpov can do...) 25 ♕g3! ♗xc1 26 ♗xb7 gives White a slight advantage as d5 is weak.

22 ♖cd1 ♘b4 23 ♕h6!

Now that the a3-f8 diagonal is blocked, White threatens 24 f6 and 25 ♕g7#.

23...♕e8 24 ♘b1! ♗b2 25 ♕d2!

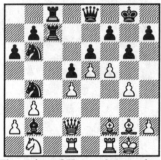

The point of Karpov's surprise retreating moves is revealed: the bishop on b2 is very awkwardly placed.

25...♘c2

25...a5? 26 a3! (26 ♕xb2?? ♖c2 27 ♕a3 ♖xa2 loses the queen) 26...♖c2 (26...♘c2 27 ♕xa5) 27 ♕e1 ♕b5 28 axb4! ♖e2 29 ♕xe2 ♕xe2 30 bxa5 ♘d7 31 ♖d2 allows White to collect rook and two bishops for the queen – a real bargain.

26 ♔h1 ♕e7 27 ♗g1 ♘d7 28 ♖f3 ♕b4 29 ♕h6!

The threats of ♖h3 and f6 drive the black queen back again. Karpov's advantage in space enables him to manoeuvre more freely than his opponent, and his superbly accurate play keeps Kamsky on the run throughout.

29...♕f8 30 ♕g5! ♕g7 31 ♕d2! b6

The black queen is stranded on g7, as 31...♕f8 loses to 32 fxe6.

32 ♖df1 a5 33 h4 ♘b4 34 a3

Of course the bishop is immune: 34 ♕xb2?? ♖c2 35 ♕a3 ♖xa2.

34...♖c2 35 ♕f4 ♘c6 36 ♗h3 ♘d8 37 ♗e3 b5 38 ♖3f2!!

Having aimed all his missiles at the black king, Karpov switches his attention to the queenside! Notice that he keeps the tension at a maximum on the kingside: a hasty f6 or fxe6 would clarify the position, allowing Black to defend more easily.

38...b4 39 axb4 axb4 40 ♖xc2 ♖xc2 41 ♖f2 ♖xf2 42 ♕xf2 ♗a3 43 ♕c2

Karpov has comprehensively outplayed his opponent: his queen controls the open c-file, while Black's pieces are all at sea. The bishop is buried alive on a3, and the knights are loose – White's immediate threat is ♕c7/c8. In desperation, Kamsky sacrifices a piece to confuse the issue.

43...♘xe5 44 dxe5 ♕xe5 45 ♕c8!

Karpov's king is exposed and his pieces are poorly placed for defence, so it would be a mistake to go passive

and try to win on material. However, this tactical blow is decisive.

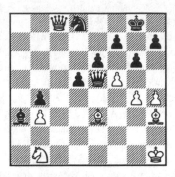

45...♕e4+ 46 ♗g2 ♕xb1+ 47 ♔h2 ♗b2 48 ♕xd8+ ♔g7 49 f6+! ♗xf6 50 ♗h6+! ♔xh6 51 ♕xf6 ♕c2 52 g5+ ♔h5 53 ♔g3!

Completing the mating net, and avoiding 53 ♔h3? ♕f5+ when Black could battle on.

53...♕c7+ 54 ♔h3 1-0

But now 54...♕c3 55 ♕xc3 bxc3 56 ♗f3# wraps up attractively.

Garry Kasparov (1963-)

Kasparov, born in Azerbaijan to parents of Jewish and Armenian extraction, was originally named Garry Vainshtein. He was seven when his father died, and adopted a russified version of Kasparian, his mother's maiden name, as soon as legally possible. Kasparov soon showed phenomenal talent, winning the USSR under-18 championship aged 12. He announced his world championship potential to the West at Banja Luka 1979, where he massacred a field which included 14 grandmasters, securing first place with three rounds to spare.

The dynamic and outspoken Kasparov was a popular successor to Karpov – who is reputed to have listed his outside interests as 'stamp-collecting and Marxism'. Kasparov's ferocious attacking play not only won favour with the public, but also stimulated his fellow grandmasters to greater endeavours, not least Karpov himself. In between title defences, Kasparov has dominated tournament chess to such an extent that in 1990 he achieved the highest FIDE rating of all time, surpassing Fischer's 1972 record. Kasparov has continually sought to professionalise chess at the top level and after the abandonment of his first match has been in almost continual conflict with the chess establishment. This conflict came to a climax with the founding of the Professional Chess Association in 1993 in the run up to the Short v Kasparov match.

8   Desert Island Chess

Computer Chess

The idea of a chess playing machine has fascinated people for centuries. The first chess automaton was designed in 1769 by Farkas Kempelen, a councillor at the Austro Hungarian court and known as The Turk.

The machine consisted of a larger than life figure, dressed in Turkish costume and seated at a wooden cabinet which took on all comers at chess. Originally designed to entertain the Empress Maria Theresa, The Turk became a huge attraction, touring Europe with its inventor from 1783 until his death in 1804. The Turk was sold and continued its travels, touring the USA from 1826 until its owner's death in 1838. The Turk then retired to a Philadelphia museum, where it perished in a fire in 1854.

Before each performance the audience was invited to inspect the machine's interior as a succession of doors and drawers were opened and closed. This was in fact the first example of the cabinet illusion, a regular in magic shows even today. Speculation as to The Turk's modus operandi caused much spilling of ink but all was revealed in 1834 when a former operator named Mouret sold his story to the *Magasin Pittoresque*.

The second famous automaton, Ajeeb, appeared in 1868 and in common with the first had the operator secreted inside. The third automaton named Mephisto was operated electro-mechanically from another room. The automata provided a regular income for some top players: Pillsbury (Ajeeb) memorably won Hastings 1895, his first major tournament, whereas Gunsberg (Mephisto) challenged Steinitz for the world championship.

The first genuine chess playing machine was invented by a Spaniard named Leonardo Torres y Quevedo. Called Ajedricista, it played the endgame of king and rook against king calculating the best move in any position and executing it automatically on the board. Ajedricista represented a critical step in the history of computing, showing that a machine could follow a programmed sequence of instructions. It is kept at the Polytechnic Museum of Madrid where it remains in full working order.

With the advent of electronic computers, chess was a natural avenue for research into expert systems and artificial intelligence. Alan Turing, one of the pioneers of computing, wrote a chess program around 1947; however he lacked access to the necessary hardware and had to perform the calculations by hand. In 1956 the scientists at Los Alamos took a break from making atomic bombs to teach their computer, Maniac, to play a mini chess game with no bishops and a 6x6 board. It managed to beat a young woman who had just learnt the rules thus securing her a place in history as the first human to lose to a computer at chess.

In 1958 an American called Alex Bernstein wrote the first program to play a full game of chess but the first to play competitively was Mac Hack VI the brainchild of Richard Greenblatt, a student at MIT. Mac Hack played its first human tournament in 1967 scoring ½/5 against weak opposition. In 1977 the program played and lost three times to Bobby Fischer—the reclusive champion's only published games between 1972 and 1992.

Undaunted, the computer experts confidently predicted that the end was nigh for human chess champions. The young Scottish Champion begged to differ and in 1968 wagered £500, half his annual salary, that no computer would beat him under tournament conditions within ten years. Levy's exposure soon doubled as two more academics entered the fray. In 1971 Ed Kozdrowicki of Bell Laboratories weighed in with another $1000. Later the same day Kozdrowicki was heard muttering something about a 'damn fool bet' after his program had produced an all-time classic of computer ineptitude.

Coko III-Genie
US Computer Ch 1971

In the position below White can of course win as he pleases, thanks to his overwhelming material advantage. To its credit, Coko spies a forced mate.

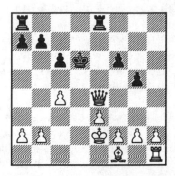

28 c5+! ♔xc5 29 ♕d4+ ♔b5 30 ♔d1+ ♔a5 31 b4+ ♔a4 32 ♕c3 ♖ed8+ 33 ♔c2

Now ♕b3# cannot be stopped, so Black delays the inevitable by giving up both rooks.

33...♖d2+ 34 ♔xd2 ♖d8+ 35 ♔c2 ♖d2+ 36 ♕xd2

This is rather strange, given that White forces mate in one after 36 ♔xd2; nevertheless, it is still mate in three.

36...♔a3 37 ♕c3+ ♔xa2

Now the fun really starts: with two instant mates to choose from, Coko appears unable to decide which one it prefers – and plays neither!

38 ♔c1? f5 39 ♔c2? f4 40 ♔c1? g4 41 ♔c2? f3 42 ♔c1? fxg2 43 ♔c2? gxh1♕

White's last six moves could perhaps be explained as a pioneering example of silicon humour, as both mates are still on. But now Coko really blows it.

44 ♔c1?? ♕xf1+ 45 ♔d2 ♕xf2+ 46 ♔c1 ♕g1+ 47 ♔c2 ♕xh2+

The queen ending is winning for Black, as the g-pawn cannot be stopped.

48 ☗c1 ♛h1+ 49 ☗c2 ♛b1+ 50 ☗d2 g3

50...♛b2+ forces the queen exchange at once, with a trivial win.

51 ♛c4+ ♛b3 52 ♛xb3+ ☗xb3 53 e4 ☗xb4 54 e5 g2 0-1

The long-awaited challenge came in 1978. Levy, by then an IM, faced Chess 4.7, a souped-up version of the world computer champion. Levy adopted a cautious policy, avoiding theoretical openings and tactics to negate the massive crunching power of the machine. Levy's superior positional knowledge and endgame technique enabled him to win the match but not before he lost one game and scrambled a draw from a lost position in another. The academics had seen it coming and paid up with good grace apart from Kozdrowicki.

Levy admitted afterwards that the moral victory belonged to the computer experts who were correct in principle but over optimistic about the time scale. The spectacular development of chip technology has continued apace and the silicon master is now a reality. A Pentium processor can examine hundreds of thousands of positions a second, which generally outweighs the poor strategic insight common to all chess programs at present.

A few seconds' thought should convince any human player that in the position below White draws trivially by shuffling around with his king. A computer would have to calculate for weeks, even months, before it would say no to the free rook.

Such positions are of course exceptional, and the computer's phenomenal calculating power becomes ever more dominant the faster the time limit. A blitz tournament at Munich 1994 saw Kasparov share first place with a computer program Fritz3 running on a 90 MHz Pentium computer. I was privileged or unfortunate enough—I do not know which—to witness this event and the shell-shocked grandmasters. Only Nigel Short took his defeat with any equanimity, declaring 'this thing is better than me at blitz'. Kasparov got the better of Fritz in a play-off but he was not so fortunate in the first round of the Intel Grand Prix at London in 1994.

Kasparov-Pentium Genius
London Intel rapid 1994
1 c4 c6 2 d4 d5 3 ♘f3 ♘f6 4 ♛c2 dxc4 5 ♛xc4 ♗f5 6 ♘c3 ♘bd7 7 g3 e6 8 ♗g2 ♗e7 9 0-0 0-0 10 e3 ♘e4 11 ♛e2 ♛b6 12 ♖d1

12 ♘d2 ♘d6 was played in Vaganian-Shirov, Manila OL 1992, when 13 b3 a5 14 ♗a3 ♖fe8 15 ♖ac1 gives White a slight advantage, according to Shirov. Kasparov tries another plan, aiming to play e4.

12...♖ad8 13 ♘e1 ♘df6 14 ♘xe4 ♘xe4 15 f3 ♘d6 16 a4 ♕b3

This is typical of the 'unnatural' moves computers tend to play in quiet positions; no human master would choose to expose his queen like this. However, in the short time available, Kasparov is unable to find an effective plan to gain the advantage.

17 e4 ♗g6 18 ♖d3 ♕b4 19 b3 ♘c8 20 ♘c2 ♕b6 21 ♗f4 c5 22 ♗e3 cxd4 23 ♘xd4 ♗c5 24 ♖ad1 e5 25 ♘c2 ♖xd3 26 ♕xd3 ♘e7 27 b4 ♗xe3+ 28 ♕xe3 ♖d8!

Taking control of the d-file; of course 29 ♕xb6?? loses to 29...♖xd1+ and 30...axb6.

29 ♖xd8+ ♕xd8 30 ♗f1 b6 31 ♕c3 f6 32 ♗c4+ ♗f7

The position is completely equal, but from here on Kasparov is completely outplayed!

33 ♘e3?

It seems wrong to allow the black queen to occupy d4, but Kasparov may still have been playing for the win. A calm move like 33 ♔f2 should hold the draw comfortably.

33...♕d4 34 ♗xf7+ ♔xf7 35 ♕b3+ ♔f8 36 ♔g2 ♕d2+ 37 ♔h3 ♕e2 38 ♘g2 h5!

Suddenly ...g5-g4+ is threatened, winning the knight or even mating in some variations. The game is now pure tactics and not even Kasparov

can cope against a computer at a fast time limit.

39 ♕e3 ♕c4 40 ♕d2 ♕e6+ 41 g4 hxg4+ 42 fxg4 ♕c4 43 ♕e1 ♕b3+ 44 ♘e3 ♕d3 45 ♔g3 ♕xe4 46 ♕d2 ♕f4+ 47 ♔g2 ♕d4 48 ♕xd4 exd4

The black queen's reign of terror is ended, but the knight ending offers no salvation − Black is simply a pawn up.

49 ♘c4 ♘c6 50 b5 ♘e5 51 ♘d6 d3 52 ♔f2 ♘xg4+ 53 ♔e1 ♘xh2 54 ♔d2 ♘f3+ 55 ♔xd3 ♔e7 56 ♘f5+

56 ♘c8+ and 57 ♘xa7 takes the knight too far away from Black's passed pawns.

56...♔f7 57 ♔e4 ♘d2+ 58 ♔d5 g5 59 ♘d6+ ♔g6 60 ♔d4 ♘b3+ 0-1

61...♘c5 would come next, when White cannot cope with the threats on both sides of the board.

Pentium Genius drew the second game, sensationally eliminating Kasparov from the tournament. The computer reached the quarter final where it came up against Vishy Anand who struck a blow back for us humans. So computers are a match for the best at 5 minute chess, even at 25 minute chess but I share Kasparov's belief that they may never overcome the very best players at normal tournament time limits. Computers have no fantasy or imagination and are too materialistic. My conversations with chess programmers suggest that they are encountering great difficulties making the computers understand more and are becoming increasingly reliant on brute force to take them forward. At a slow time limit a top GM can think longer term and outplay any computer strategically he just has to avoid the 'cheapos' admittedly an exceedingly difficult task. While the computers are crunching away, a GM considers a minimal number of moves but most of them are good moves. A computer that could mimic a GM's intuition would surely be invincible but this seems a long way off. Nevertheless, computers can already defeat 99.9999% of all players.

A better yardstick than speed chess tournaments is the annual Aegon Computer v Human tournament. Humans ranging from club player to GM play an assortment of top computer programs. The 1995 edition saw the computers win overall but the individual contest was won by John van der Wiel, an experienced Dutch GM. He explained afterwards that the humans' biggest mistake was that they tried to play 'real' chess. He adapted his style to beat the computers.

Hiarcs-Van der Wiel
The Hague AEGON 1995
1 e4 e6 2 d4 d5 3 ♘c3 ♗b4 4 e5 b6
This move indicates Black's desire to exchange off his bad light-squared bishop at the first opportunity. The dour positional battle that generally ensues gives the human GM good chances to exploit the computer's lack of aptitude for long-range planning.
5 ♕g4 ♗f8
A curious-looking move to the uninitiated, but Black wishes to defend

g7 without weakening his pawn structure.
6 ♗g5 ♕d7 7 h4 h6 8 ♗f4 ♗a6 9 ♗xa6 ♘xa6 10 ♘f3 ♘e7 11 0-0?
Black has already achieved his strategic objective without difficulty, but this simply castles into Black's planned attack on the king-side-perhaps nobody had told Hiarcs that it shouldn't castle where the pawn cover is compromised.
11...♘f5 12 a3 ♘b8 13 h5 ♘c6 14 ♖fd1 ♖g8
Black makes as many useful moves as possible before castling. The computer does not realise it should attack on the queenside until the king actually goes there, so it wastes valuable time drifting planlessly.
15 ♔h2 0-0-0 16 b4
Finally getting the message, but Black's attack is ready to roll.
16...♗e7 17 ♕h3 g5 18 hxg6 fxg6 19 g4 ♘g7 20 ♗xh6
Only a computer could be this greedy, opening the h-file where its king and queen are conveniently lined up!
20...♖h8 21 b5 ♘a5 22 ♖h1 ♖h7 23 ♔g2 ♖dh8 24 g5 ♘f5 25 a4 ♘c4 26 ♘e2 ♗xg5
Pulling the rug from under White's feet.
27 ♘xg5 ♖xh6 28 ♕c3 ♕e7 29 ♘f3 ♕h7 30 ♖xh6 ♕xh6 31 ♘eg1 ♕f4 32 ♔f1 g5 33 a5
A belated attempt at counterplay.
33...bxa5 34 ♖xa5 ♘xa5 35 ♕xa5 ♔b8 0-1.
The threats of ...g4 and ...♘xd4 are decisive.

Chess Databases & Training with your Computer

Nearly every top player nowadays has a computer containing a database program with hundreds of thousands of games. The most popular of these programs is ChessBase, developed by a German, Matthias Wüllenweber, who responded to a call by Garry Kasparov in 1986 for someone to invent a method of chess game storage and retrieval. Chess databases allow the top players to seek out games played by and then prepare for, prospective opponents. For the amateur player with a PC or Mac, chess databases are a valuable source of study material. Games can be classified by opening, year, tournament even by the exact position and so anyone can compare his play with that of the masters. Recent developments allow you to seek out positional themes such as doubled pawns or tactical motifs such as the Greek Bishop Sacrifice in Chapter 2. Training with a chess database and a computer chess playing opponent is sure to improve your chess or just give you hours of fun browsing through the games of the masters. A word of warning: when using a database for serious study, concentrate on material with explanations and analysis. Endlessly playing through scores of unannotated games is of little use.

Challenge your electronic playing partner to games in your chosen openings and use it to check your assessment of positions.

While writing this book I used Genius 3 and Fritz 3 to check a lot of published analysis; the silicon beasts discovered lots of mistakes, even by top players.

Chess on the Internet

With the advent of the information super-highway there is now a global chess club whose doors never close, boasting a membership of thousands, from social players to strong GMs. Real live opponents on tap at any hour of the day or night. Playing chess with real mistakes and real excitement... and all in the comfort of your own home. These are the joys of chess on the Internet. Once you have registered and installed the right software, you will have a chess board diagram on which you mouse-click your moves and your opponent's appear automatically. Time limits are open to negotiation but blitz chess with a Fischer-style increment is most popular. Once you have entered your move it is considered made and cannot be retracted in a rated game. Disconnecting in a lost position is considered the height of bad manners!

Thousands of games are played each day and there about 50 titled players on the Internet Chess Club, which pays the pros to give lectures and host discussion forums. You can watch and pass comment on any game or have 20 games of a selected opponent e-mailed to you. In the future you will be able to see and talk to your opponents as well.

There are also lots of chess sites on the World Wide Web. My *DT* articles and those of David Norwood can be found on *The Chess Connection*, an electronic chess magazine. Other sites hold discussions and allow you to download games.

Correspondence Chess

If you live a long way from the nearest chess club, or simply enjoy taking your time over your moves, then correspondence chess is an excellent way to improve your game. There are several correspondence clubs to choose from (details at the end of the chapter) and all of them have tournaments for all standards. You can also play against people in other countries. There is a little administrative work involved. You can transmit moves by postcard or use specially designed scorecards. On each card write you move and the number of days taken to reply. Always keep a separate record of the complete game in case a move is lost. A typical rate of play is 10 moves every 20 days each—leisurely enough for most. Days are measured by the time taken between the day the move is received and the reply postmarked. The biggest frustration, particularly for international competitors, is the time moves spend in transit. The final of the World Correspondence Championships takes several years to compete. Indeed, the East German team were still playing the Correspondence Chess Olympiad years after the Berlin Wall came down and Germany had been unified!

This will change as soon as CC players make use of e-mail, eliminating the cost of postage and delay in transmission and promising a bright future for correspondence chess.

Chess Composition

Chess players have been composing positions for instruction and entertainment for hundreds of years producing a huge body of work of which we can barely scratch the surface here. The two main categories of chess composition are problems and studies. In a problem the desired result must be achieved within a stated number of moves, whereas the object of a study is either a win or a draw, the number of moves in the solution having no significance.

Chess Problems

Chess problems originated in medieval Europe with the requirement to give mate in a specified number of moves. Nowadays a chess problem might include non-checking 'quiet' key moves, alternatives for Black (generally the fall guy in compositions) and economical use of material. These standards lie at the foundation of the problemist's edifice, which today comprises a bewildering array of themes with a jargon to match. The brilliant American composer Sam Loyd was undoubtedly the greatest publicist the genre has had: he avoided the obscure technicalities and created positions that have puzzled and entertained solvers for well over a century. No matter what the stipulation, chess problems strip away the positional assessments, struggle and uncertainty from the practical game, leaving just the glistening core of pure logic.

Loyd, Boston Gazette 1859

White to play and mate in two moves

1 ♕a5!

This does not threaten anything in particular, but places Black in zugzwang - a remarkable feat, given the large number of pieces on the board. In addition, the white queen swinging the full width of the board is a nice geometrical touch. Every black defensive try fails, for the following reasons:

1...♗d7 or 1...♗d6 blocks the d-file, allowing 2 ♕d5#.

1...♗e7 or 1...♗e6 blocks the e-file, allowing 2 ♕e5#.

1...♖e7 or 1...♖d6, blocking the f8-bishop, or 1...♗g7 or 1...♗h6, moving it away, allow 2 ♕xb4#.

1...♖d7 or 1...♖e6 blocks the c8-bishop, while 1...♗b7 permits 2 ♘f5#.

1...♖d5 2 ♕xd5#, 1...♖e5 2 ♕xe5# and 1...♗f5 2 ♘xf5# also fail.

Finally, 1...♗c5 blocks a vital escape square for the king in the event of 2 ♕a1#.

Studies

A study is usually an endgame position, where White either wins or draws in seemingly impossible circumstances. Studies are closer to real games than problems, pure tactics as opposed to pure logic. Fantastic, paradoxical ideas take centre stage: no less a player than Kasparov has advocated solving problems and studies as a means to develop a larger 'vocabulary' of tactical ideas and a heightened aesthetic sensibility.

Chess Literature

There is no short-cut to chess mastery. To play the opening well requires a knowledge of specific moves *and* of general principles and typical strategies. There is no shortage of superb chess literature to choose from, but use it wisely. If you want to improve your game, read about all aspects of the game and not just the opening. Look out for books and magazines where the top players annotate their own games. Studying the endgame will probably yield more rating points per hour than anything else, so take Karpov's advice and do it! Read critically and take nothing for granted as even the best authors make mistakes—while the worst do it deliberately to mislead future opponents. No matter how modest your pretensions as a player, whatever time you give to chess will be amply rewarded by the beauty of the game alone.

Recommended Reading

My 60 Memorable Games	Fischer
John Nunn's Best Games	Nunn
Steve Davis Plays Chess	Davis & Norwood
Batsford Chess Openings 2	Kasparov & Keene
Secrets of Spectacular Chess	Levitt & Friedgood
Complete Chess Strategy 1,2 & 3	Pachman (second hand only)
Garry Kasparov's Fighting Chess	Kasparov, Speelman & Wade
Think Like a Grandmaster	Kotov
Chess Openings	Basman
How to Reassess Your Chess	Silman
My System	Nimzowitsch
Chess the Adventurous Way	Timman
Practical Chess Endings	Keres
Tactics for Advanced Players	Averbakh
My Life in Chess	Gufeld
The Even More Complete Chess Addict	Fox & James
Comprehensive Chess Course	Pelts & Alburt
Positional Chess Handbook	Gelfer
Planning	McDonald
Gambits	Burgess
Piece Power	Wells
Pawn Power	Dunnington
Opening Play	Ward
Chess for Tigers	Webb
Art of Attack in Chess	Vukovic
How Good is Your Chess	King

Chess as a Spectator Sport

You might think that the prospect of spending up to eight hours in total silence watching a game of chess is fairly unappealing, let alone paying for the privilege—and of course you'd be right. The way forward has been shown by the PCA with their Speed Chess Grand Prix tournaments sponsored by Intel.

Chess *can* be presented attractively. Knockout matches and blitz chess play-offs are an attractive format. The problem of communicating the moves to a large audience is solved by an 'intelligent' sensory chess board that recognises the pieces electronically, transmitting the game position to monitors in parts of the theatre or to a big screen. Spectators can listen to expert commentary by means of radio headsets; the only problem occurs when the commentators are a little too entertaining and laughter from the audience disturbs the players. As a regular in the commentary box I have been guilty on occasion of disturbing the peace and once received the equivalent of the red card from the arbiter. Close-ups of the players' faces, the board and the clock add the finishing touches to the PCA roadshow, which has played to packed houses in New York, London, Paris and most spectacularly of all, the Palace of Congresses in the heart of the Kremlin.

Useful Addresses

National Federations & Associations

British Chess Federation: 9a Grand Parade, St Leonards on Sea, East Sussex TN38 0DD. 01424 442500
Scottish Chess Association: 40 Criffell Rd, Glasgow G32 0SB.
Welsh Chess Union: Furzeland, Trimsaran Rd, Llanelli, Dyfed, SA15 4RN.
Irish Chess Union: 115 Sandyhill Gdns, Ballynum, Dublin 11.
United States Chess Federation: 186 Route 9W, New Windsor, NY 12550-7698. 1-800-KING
British Women's Chess Association: Hawthorn Cottage, Market St, Tunstead, Norfolk, NR12 8AH.
British Chess Problem Society: 76 Albany Drive, Herne Bay, Kent, CT6 8SJ.

Correspondence Chess

BCCA: 6 Batchelors Way, Chesham, Bucks, HP5 2 DU.
BCCS: Quince House, 79 St Neots Rd, Sandy, Beds, SG19 1LQ.
Postal Chess League: 1 Norbury Rise, London SW16 4JF.

Chess Supplies

Chess & Bridge Ltd: 369 Euston Rd, London NW1 3AR. 0171 388 2404
ManCHESSter Supplies: 25 School Grove, Prestwich, Manchester M25 9RJ. 0161 773 6294
Chess Supplies Scotland: 15 Hope St, Glasgow G2 6AQ. 0141 248 2887
USCF: 186 Route 9W, New Windsor, NY 12550-7698. 1-800-KING
Chess Digest: P. O. Box 59029, Dallas Texas, 75229. 1-800-462-3548

Chess Magazines

CHESS Monthly: 369 Euston Rd, London NW1 3AR. 0171 388 2404. Editor: M.Pein
Kingpin: 45b Empress Ave, Ilford, Essex, IG1 3DE: 0181 554 8266. Editor: J.Manley
B.C.M.: 69 Masbro Rd, London W14 0LS: 0171 603 2877. Editor: M.Chandler
New in Chess: P. O. Box 3053, 1801 GB Alkmaar. +31 72 127137. Editor. J.Timman
Inside Chess: P. O. Box 19457, Seattle, WA. Editor: Y.Seirawan

Chess on the Internet

Internet Chess Club: telnet chess.lm.com 5000 or telnet 192.231.221.16 5000
FICS: telnet ics.onenet.net 5000 or telnet 164.58.253.10 5000
The Chess Connection: http://WWW.easynet.co.uk/pages/world-chess/home.htm
The Week in Chess by Mark Crowther has a link from The Chess Connection

Chess Coaching

Association of Chess Tutors: 10 Ruvigny Mansions, Embankment, London SW15 1LE
Chess & Bridge Ltd: as above
BCF: as above
USCF: as above
BCF: as above

Openings Checklist

I. **Open Games:**

1 e4 e5

2 d4	Centre Game	
2 ♗c4	Bishop's Opening	
2 f4	King's Gambit	
2 ♘c3	Vienna Game	

2 ♘f3

2...f5	Latvian Gambit	
2...d6	Philidor Defence	
2...♘f6	Petroff Defence [Russian Game]	

2...♘c6

3 c3	Ponziani Opening	
3 ♘c3 ♘f6	Four Knights' Opening	
3 d4	Scotch Opening	

3 ♗c4

3...♗e7	Hungarian Defence
3...♘f6	Two Knights' Defence
3...♗c5	Giuoco Piano

3 ♗b5   Ruy Lopez [Spanish Opening]

II. **Semi-Open Games:**

1 e4

1...b6	Owen's Defence
1...♘c6	Nimzowitsch Defence
1...d5	Scandinavian Defence [Centre Counter]
1...♘f6	Alekhine's Defence
1...d6	Pirc Defence
1...g6	Modern Defence
1...c6	Caro-Kann Defence
1...e6	French Defence
1...c5	Sicilian Defence

III.   **Queen's Gambit**

1 d4 d5
> 2 ♘c3   Richter-Veresov

2 c4
> 2...e5   Albin Counter-Gambit
> 2...♗f5   Baltic Defence
> 2...♘c6   Chigorin Defence
> 2...c6   Slav Defence
> 2...dxc4   Queen's Gambit Accepted
> 2...e6 3 ♘c3
>> 3...c5   Tarrasch Defence
>> 3...e6
>>> 4 cxd5   Exchange Variation
>>> 4 ♘f3
>>>> 4...c5   Semi-Tarrasch
>>>> 4...c6   Semi-Slav
>>> 4 ♗g5 ♗e7 5 e3   Orthodox QGD

IV.   **Indian Defences**

1 d4 f5   Dutch Defence
1 d4 ♘f6
> 2 ♗g5   Trompowski Opening
> 2 c4
>> 2...e5   Budapest Defence
>> 2...d6   Old Indian Defence
>> 2...c5 3 d5
>>> 3...e5   Czech Benoni
>>> 3...e6   Modern Benoni
>>> 3...b5   Benko Gambit
>> 2...g6 3 ♘c3
>>> 3...d5   Grünfeld Defence
>>> 3...♗g7   King's Indian Defence
>> 2...e6
>>> 3 g3 d5   Catalan Opening
>>> 3 ♘c3 ♗b4 Nimzo-Indian Defence
> 3 ♘f3
>> 3...c5 4 d5 b5   Blumenfeld Gambit
>> 3...♗b4+   Bogo-Indian Defence
>> 3...b6   Queen's Indian Defence

V.   **Flank Openings**

1 g4   Grob Opening
1 b4   Sokolsky Opening
1 f4   Bird's Opening
1 b3   Nimzowitsch-Larsen Attack
1 ♘f3   Réti Opening and King's Indian Attack
1 c4   English Opening